THE PERSONAL SUCCESS HANDBOOK

Also by Antony J. Iozzi

The Personal Success Handbook—Unabridged
*—for leaders, managers and supervisors, and
anyone in charge of others*

The Sales Success Handbook
*—your guide to the systems and strategies
of highly effective sales people*

The Nine Pillars of Happiness
*—the suspense thriller for
the new millennium—(a novel)*

THE
PERSONAL SUCCESS HANDBOOK

HOW TO ACHIEVE PERSONAL EXCELLENCE

AND LEAD YOURSELF TO WEALTH, HEALTH AND HAPPINESS

Authors Choice Press
San Jose New York Lincoln Shanghai

The Personal Success Handbook
How to Achieve Personal Excellence, and Lead yourself to Wealth, Health and Hapiness

Authors Choice Press
an imprint of iUniverse.com, Inc.

For information address:
iUniverse.com, Inc.
620 North 48th Street, Suite 201
Lincoln, NE 68504-3467
www.iuniverse.com

Originally published by The Business Library

ISBN: 0-595-13331-2

Printed in the United States of America

DEDICATION

To my parents, Orazio and Maria.

Their hard work, love, persistence and dedication to building a better future has always been an inspiration to me.

They have achieved success through a high standard of Personal Excellence.

With love and thanks I dedicate The Personal Success Handbook to them.

Acknowledgments

This Personal Success Handbook is a collection of my own experiences and the wisdom, experiences and inspiration of people far too many to list here.

To all who have contributed to my knowledge of the dynamics or personal success I offer my heartfelt thanks.

For ease of reading the he pronoun is used throughout. However the he and she pronouns are interchangeable.

Also, all names used in examples are fictitious.

About the Author

In a career spanning some 30 years, Tony Iozzi has amassed success experiences as a businessman, consultant to government, lecturer at the Air Force's Officers Training School, public relations consultant, marketer, sales manager, sales trainer, salesman, public speaker and motivator.

In designing and providing unique training and personal development programmes to businesses and individuals, he is fulfilling his aim of helping others achieve wealth, health and happiness through Self leadership and Personal Excellence.

Foreword

When many people think of success they usually think of money; lots of it. To be sure, money is essential, and it is our duty to acquire it. Having it shows we have succeeded in the Financial Sphere of life. But what of the Family, Personal, Work, Community and Spiritual Spheres?

We cannot all be billionaire entrepreneurs and no person or course should pretend otherwise. However to the extent we wish to strive for it we are all empowered to achieve and live a successful life.

The Personal Success Handbook proclaims the philosophy of **Wholistic** success. Wealth? Certainly! But with health and happiness.

By tapping the centuries-old vein of success experience The Personal Success Handbook shows the how, not just the what, of living success.

It is a work with a mission. It's reason for being is to foster and nourish the principles of **success through Self leadership and Personal Excellence.**

Until now you might have been living a storyline written for you by someone else. You might need to script your own destiny; to live life by design, not by default; by plan, not by accident.

What kind of storyline would you write for your life if you knew you **couldn't** fail?

The best of everything could lie ahead of you. Let The Personal Success Handbook help you fulfil the promise of your better future.

A. J. IOZZI

Contents

BOOK TWO

APPLIED SUCCESS KNOWLEDGE AND SKILLS

Book One

Success Knowledge

1

The Moment You Change Your Life Forever

We do not have secret police keeping people from success and happiness. We do not have a bureau to prevent citizens from claiming their share of wealth. What we have right now are billions of dollars circulating all around us.

Yet amid this wealth Tom and Mary spend hours foraging for specials to save one dollar! They buy a second rate item to save ten cents.

They might be honest, loyal and good taxpayers but live from day to day in dread of the next bill; paupers in the midst of wealth.

In the end they will retire at the mercy of a State pension.

Were Tom and Mary conditioned into poverty? Were they given storylines on how to live their life; storylines written by others?

Conditioners such as "Money can't buy happiness," "There are more important things than money" and "Money is the root of all evil" (which should be "The *love* of money is the root of all evil") contribute to many people's financial downfall. (Other reasons will be discussed later).

How concerned should Tom and Mary have been about creating wealth? If they had seen life as it is and not as they thought it should be, what choices could they have made?

A survey showed that of 100 people starting out, by age 65*

30 are already dead

Only 7 live on more than $653 per week (gross)

50 live on incomes between $125 per week and $653 per week (the median is $253 per week)

13 live on less than $125 per week (poverty level)

(*Australian Bureau of Statistics; 1988)

Yet the June 1992 issue of Business Review Weekly showed that of Australia's wealthiest 400 families, only some two percent inherited their wealth. The others made it!

Obviously the 98 percent were very concerned about creating wealth. But what factors made the difference?

Given the choice, most people would choose wealth over poverty. The problem is that most people don't realise wealth *is* a matter of choice

It isn't society, God, the Government, the 'System', the weather, anyone or anything which prevents people from living a financially successful life. What shapes their destiny are the choices and decisions they make each day.

Tom and Mary were empowered to choose success. They were empowered to learn how to succeed in all the six spheres of life, but chose otherwise.

In the *financial* sphere of life, Tom and Mary's security was limited to the support provided by their community.

Were they successful?

Bill and Helen would not think so. They devoted most of their energy to the avid pursuit of wealth. Both had professional careers (which unfortunately reduced the time they could spend with their children).

Bill became adept at investing in shares and property. By the time they were in their early forties they had accumulated enough money to generate an independent income for life. But they had even bigger goals.

By now their two boys were 18 and 21 and had lived away from home ever since that terrible row a year ago. Bill and Helen simply don't understand young people these days. Hadn't they provided their boys with the best that money could buy?

Were Bill and Helen successful?

Brenda and Jason would not think so. They doted on their three children. In their fifties, they enjoy a close relationship with all their children regardless of age (the youngest is eleven).

Brenda thinks that being a wife and mother is the most important job in the world. Jason earns a modest income as an electrician. His plans for securing his future will come to fruition at retirement. Financially, he will have put away enough money to supplement his pension, but no more.

Are Brenda and Jason successful?

Terence Lewis might not think so. He seemed to have everything; wealth, power, position, respect and a high regard as a valued member of the community of Queensland, Australia. He was Commissioner of Police; the State's top cop. In 1991 he was found guilty of corruption and is serving a long prison sentence.

Was he successful?

Brian Epstein, the man who created Beatlemania and launched the Beatles as the most famous pop group in history added great wealth to his already full purse. He had an impeccable upbringing, fame, youth, glamour and wealth and managed three of the most successful pop groups in the world. Yet he 'lived on pills'; pills to help him sleep, pills to wake him up, pills to cheer him up. At the early age of 32, the man envied by the world's impresarios died from a self-administered accidental overdose of drugs. (From: Brian Epstein, 'The Man Who Made The Beatles' by Ray Coleman)

Was Brian Epstein successful?

Elvis Presley was idolised and adored by millions. Referred to as 'The King' his legend refuses to die. He achieved fame, wealth and power, yet in 1967 Elvis tried to take his own life by swallowing a whole bottle of barbiturates.

Bloated and unhappy, Elvis was dependent on drugs to the end. The Biochemist who investigated Elvis's death said he had never seen so many drugs in one specimen. (From: 'Elvis: the Last 24 Hours' by Albert Goldman)

Was Elvis Presley successful?

John Spencer would certainly not think so. John is a lay preacher and part time missionary. All his work is devoted to charitable causes and, hence, produces little income for himself.

John has a deep conviction that God will provide for his needs.

Is John successful?

Terry White might think so. Terry was encouraged by all his friends and his wife to become a salesman because people liked him and sought his advice.

However all he knew was how to be a good sheet metal worker. He dreaded paperwork and "Wasn't any good with numbers".

Persuaded, Terry became a Life Insurance Salesman. His wife Laura helped with administration and the two made a great team.

Everyone was right! In his first year Terry won all the awards and trebled his former income. Then one night he attempted suicide, saved only by a chance visit from a friend he hadn't seen for two years.

Was he a success?

These are questions for you to answer. But before you do it's important to remember that we all live in a number of spheres, and judging anyone by taking into account only one part of his life simply doesn't provide a complete answer.

How Many Lives Do You Live?

Have you ever listed the many lives you live? Have you ever asked yourself how successful you wanted to be in each life?

Your work life - and the way you behave at work is probably quite different to your home life and your behaviour at home. Your community life is probably different again.

Imagine that a trusted friend made arrangements for you to visit a television studio as members of an audience for a popular show. You sit in the front row, casting your eyes at the props, the lights, the cables strewn on the floor linking the television cameras....

Suddenly there is an eruption of applause. The popular host - whose face you recognise at once - walks briskly to the centre in front of an elaborate settee. His trained voice fills the studio as he looks straight at you and cries:

"This is your life!"

You freeze. Why you? Your friend pats you on the back and smiles, joining the audience in even louder applause as he encourages you to take your place before the cameras.

The host walks towards you with outstretched hand.

"My God!" you exclaim as you walk to the settee. You sit self-consciously for what seems an eternity as the host calls friends, acquaintances and family members, each to tell their version of your life story to the world.

In your **Personal Life** would you want them to speak of your honesty, integrity, caring and self-leadership? Your success through Personal Excellence?

In your Family Life would you want them to tell the world about a loving friend, father and husband who worked to foster a happy home?

In your Financial Life would you want them to glow with admiration at the financial security you achieved for yourself and those you love?

In your Business/Work Life would you want them to tell the audience and your family about the example you set, the diligence, the support you give others?

In your Community Life would you want the guest to tell of your support for worthy causes, of your work for youth, sport and a caring community?

In your Spiritual Life would you want them to say how your work enriched the community in which you live and provided a role model for others?

'Success' in any one sphere is only part of the equation. It's like being part of a person. This handbook deals with *'Wholistic'* success; with attaining the success you want in all the six spheres of life.

How successful you will be and what you do to achieve it will depend in large part on how you perceive the world around you.

In his great book; 'The Adventures of Don Quixote De La Mancha' Miguel De Cervantes creates a pathetic yet lovable character who sets out to right the 'Unrightable wrong', 'Defend the helpless', 'Reach the unreachable star'.

The legend of Knights, chivalry, purity and great deeds were Don Quixote's reality.

Through his mind's eye he transfigures a windmill into a monster and charges at it with tilted lance (with predictable results). A scullery maid and prostitute becomes his 'Dulcinea' to whom he will dedicate his awesome victories. A run down inn becomes a castle; a barber's bowl - the mystical 'Helmet of Mandrino'.

Despite heroic efforts, Don Quixote fails to realise his splendid vision and dies in delusion. He was the very embodiment of a *Positive Mental Attitude* - yet this did not make any difference to the outcome.

He put in *'That extra effort'*, yet failed just the same. He 'read all the books' but died a broken - yet lovable - fool. He was a paragon of *self-motivation,* yet he might as well have stayed at home.

Even though he changed his life forever by becoming a 'Knight Errant', those vital success disciplines failed him.

Why?

From the start Don Quixote's quest was doomed because he followed a defective blueprint. Through his mind's eye he saw the world as he thought it was or wished it to be, not as it really existed. All the Positive Mental Attitude, extra effort, self-motivation and study simply ensured he got to the wrong place faster.

On the other hand Tom and Mary, Bill and Helen, Brenda and Jason, Terence Lewis, John Spencer, Terry White, Brian Epstein and Elvis Presley might well have seen the world as it really was, yet each achieved success in only one or a few spheres of life.

To succeed in all the major spheres of life; (Personal, Family, Business/Work, Financial, Community and Spiritual,) could require a major shift in perception; a different way of seeing things.

When we change *how* we see things we change *what* we see and our attitude and feelings towards it.

During the 'Cold War' thousands, perhaps millions of people in the West lost sleep through worry of a Soviet nuclear strike. Yet during that period the same people would not have been concerned about American, British or French nuclear weapons at all. Why? Were Western nuclear weapons any less horrific?

The difference lay in how they saw things. The Soviets were perceived as the Enemy, whilst America, Britain and France were seen as friends. What they saw, their attitude and feelings towards it and what they did about it depended on how they saw it.

Has your perception of the 'Nuclear threat' changed now the Berlin Wall has crumbled, East Europe is free from Communism and the Soviet Union disbanded?

For many centuries people perceived the world as flat. Mediterranean seamen refused to sail past the 'Pillars of Hercules' (the Strait of Gibraltar) for fear of falling off the Earth.

What happened once the flat Earth perception changed? Was not a new world discovered?

You might remember the story of a mother whose face was terribly disfigured by fire. Her teenage daughter was ashamed of her. She was embarrassed to bring her friends to her house and did not want to be seen with her mother in public.

Eventually the shame and embarrassment burst into an argument where the daughter told her mother how "ugly" she was and that she wished she had no mother at all.

One day she learned how her mother became disfigured. When the daughter was only two years old the house caught fire. Her mother risked her life again and again to save her daughter, and in the process suffered horrible burns.

This new perception transformed each scar on her mother's face into a testament of love, selflessness and devotion.

Once the daughter's perception changed, so did her attitude, feelings and behaviour. By changing *how* she saw, she changed *what* she saw.

This principle also applies to daily life. For example when I lived in an apartment some years ago, I was frequently disturbed by the noise in the apartment above mine. I put up with this for many months without complaint.

One day the noise of a masonry drill vibrated through the walls of the entire block, beginning at 7am. This was too much!

Angrily rehearsing what I would say I took the elevator to the upper floor and marched down the corridor. As I drew nearer the noise reverberated even more loudly.

I pounded on the door, ready to blast away.

When the door opened, a frail old man in a wheelchair answered:

"Yes?"

All I could say was *"Sorry, I'm from the apartment below. Do you know where that terrible noise is coming from?"*

He replied: *"I thought it was from you"*.

I had acted according to my perception, which was entirely wrong. When my perception changed so did my feelings and behaviour.

Many 'born again' Christians tell of the moment when all at once everything made sense, when they saw the 'big picture'. Their perception of the world changed and with it they changed their life forever. Charles Colson, former White House staffer and 'hatchet man' for President Richard Nixon, is an example of this. I am another example (in a spiritual, rather than religious sense.)

Yet an accurate perception of the world and your place in it will not, of itself, create the moment you change your life forever.

The Power of Dissatisfaction

Once you sharpen your perception and see the world as it really is, you could be dissatisfied with what you see. You might realise all your hard work has been railroading you towards the wrong destination.

Dissatisfaction can be a great impetus for positive change, provided it is proactive. You have the ability to empower dissatisfaction to change your life for the better.

This requires Self leadership.

Many people who do not succeed might fail because they become too satisfied. Somehow they adjust and accept their condition. They give up. If they become dissatisfied they focus on *reactive dissatisfaction*. They grumble, mumble and complain but keep living a storyline written by others or by circumstances.

If they do attend success seminars they are largely drawn by the hope of learning the secret of creating wealth quickly - preferably without working for it.

Like Tom and Mary, they do not empower *proactive dissatisfaction* to change their life for the better. They have not cried; *Enough!*

Josiah Wedgewood cried *Enough!* When the father of the woman he loved declared Sarah would never marry a Burslem potter.

Despite a painful limp, pock-marked face and nothing but years of toil as his heritage Josiah determined to achieve Personal Excellence.

Eventually he transformed his poverty stricken village into a prosperous haven for artisans, was appointed potter to the Queen of England, married Sarah, became known as the finest potter in all England and amassed a fortune. Today 'Wedgewood' is synonymous with finest quality porcelain.

Charles Dickens cried *Enough!* When his parents were put into a debtors' prison and he had to work under appalling conditions packaging shoe blackener.

He never forgot the humility his family endured, nor the exploitation of children in exhausting and degrading work.

Through books such as 'Oliver Twist' he pricked the conscience of England and changed the world forever. His works have been ranked as second only to those of Shakespeare.

James L. Kraft cried *Enough!* When his debt ridden parents could not pay the mortgage on their farm and the bank threatened to foreclose.

All young James had was an old horse and some meager savings. Yet he was determined to achieve Personal Excellence.

He peddled cheese to pay off his parent's mortgage and built the foundation for the giant Kraft Foods Group.

George Washington Carver cried *Enough!* When he saw a racist mob beat a negro to death and burn the body in the public square.

The son of slaves, George never knew his family. Yet his proactive dissatisfaction with the lot of the American Negro inspired him to refuse offers of comfort and wealth so he could advance the cause of his people.

Among other things he discovered how to make rubber from peanuts, plastic from soybeans and flour from sweet potatoes. He was known as the wizard of farm chemistry.

Gustav Dalen cried *Enough!* When he refused to live the storyline written for him by others. He realised that life on the farm would not enable him to achieve his mission.

Winner of the Nobel Prize for Physics, he revolutionised lighthouses around the world and saved countless lives.

Although blinded through his work, he invented a stove still sold today that cooks and heats for 24 hours on a small amount of coal.

Jane Addams cried *Enough!* When she saw for the first time how the poor really lived. Crippled with typhoid, tuberculosis and a curved spine Jane won a Nobel Peace Prize. She founded Hull House in Chicago's slums and devoted her life to working with the poor.

Florence Nightingale cried *Enough!* When she saw the shocking conditions of hospital treatment and hygiene.

Single-handedly she set about establishing the nursing profession and provided the foundation of today's hospital nursing system.

Violetta Chamorro cried *Enough!* When the violence which swept her country took her husband's life and threatened anarchy.

Never imagining she would be anything but a housewife and mother, she became President of Nicaragua and the first female national leader in the history of Central America.

Professor Fred Hollows cried *Enough!* When he visited Watti Creek in Outback Australia and saw how appalling eye health was among Aborigines.

"Third World stuff! Nineteenth century!" he exclaimed.

Two years and 250,000 kilometres later his trachoma programme had already made a great difference, benefiting over 100,000 Aborigines.

He established eye care hospitals and lens factories in war-torn Eritrea and restored sight to countless people.

He was crowned 'Australian of the Year' and 'Humanitarian of the Year'. His achievements are all the more remarkable when one considers Professor Hollows suffered from cancer.

Those are but a few examples of people who achieved Personal Excellence through empowering *proactive dissatisfaction.* Every day in your own community there are others who are transforming their future by crying; *Enough!*

Dr Donald A Laird, author of 'The Technique of Getting Things Done' discovered that dissatisfaction tied to a specific goal is a powerful incentive to action.

The power to change is always within us. It cannot be taken from us unless we surrender it.

Unfortunately, for many people the impetus of dissatisfaction is fleeting. Before long they adjust, they accept, they acquiesce and live the storyline written by others. And that is so easy to do. Just as in a sealed room one gets accustomed to stale air. After a while you don't notice it at all, and forget about it. Eventually you think this is the way it is; you don't believe anything else. You defend it.

All it takes is for a crack to let in a breath of fresh air. Only then do you realise what fresh air is. As a result you become dissatisfied with what you have and yearn to breathe fresh air and freedom.

Yet the moment of dissatisfaction alone is not the moment you change your life forever. Proactive dissatisfaction is the starter motor that gets your engine for change going.

The Moment You Change Your Life Forever

It is most likely that the moment you change your life forever will be an experience unique to you. In analysing it you will be able to trace it to a number of events which paved the way to that particular point in time.

Realising the importance of creating wealth, of itself, will not bring the moment about. Humans are deeper than placing all their values on money. We need social contact, affection, respect, to be appreciated, a sense of importance and more.

Identifying your spheres of life and determining to succeed in all or some of them will not bring the moment of change either. Recognising the various lives you live and the impact you have on those around you is a fine beginning, but not a result.

Gaining accurate perceptions so you change your frame of reference; that too is important, but not of itself because knowledge unapplied is of little value.

Empowering proactive dissatisfaction gets us very close, but dissatisfaction can pass, then we adjust, acquiesce, accept.

Rounding your life's goal with a mission will provide purpose, direction and self-esteem, but will not be the moment you change your life forever.

Consider the moment when a particular young man who was destined to become known throughout the world, changed his life forever.

Wearing a smart business suit and a turban he bought a first class rail ticket in 1893 South Africa and took his seat.

The burly conductor looked aghast. He demanded the young man go to the third class carriage. When the young man refused, showing the conductor the first class ticket, the conductor threw him bodily from the train.

Angry and frustrated, the young lawyer wanted to leave that country. Then he asked himself the question;

"Should I run away, or stay to fight injustice even though it will mean personal harm?"

Dusting off his suit he walked back to the platform, sat down and waited for the next train. He had *committed* to stay and fight and in so doing changed his life - and the history of South Africa and India - forever.

His name? Mohandas Gandhi. He too cried *Enough!*

The moment you change your life forever comes at the culmination of all your self-discoveries; when they coalesce and enable you to see the big picture. In an instant you *commit*, deep down in your heart, to a set of core values and a path for your life's work that you will follow regardless of the frustrations, setbacks and pain along the way.

The moment of *commitment* to live your life by design in a way that enriches you and the community, that is the moment you *begin* to change you life forever.

W.N. Murray of the 1951 Scottish Himalayan Expedition has this to say about commitment:

"Until one is committed there is hesitancy, the chance to draw back, always ineffectiveness. Concerning all acts of initiative (and creation) there is one elemental truth, the ignorance of which kills countless ideas and splendid plans.

"The moment one definitely commits oneself, then providence moves too. All sorts of things occur to help one that would never otherwise have occurred. A whole stream of events issues from the decision, raising in one's favour all manner of unforeseen incidents and meetings and material assistance, which no man could have dreamt would have come his way.

"I have learned a deep respect for one of Goethe's couplets;

"Whatever you can do, or dream you can, begin it. Boldness has genius, power and magic in it. "

You *want* success! True success; the kind of success that cannot be measured by dollars alone.

Intuitively you have recognised that to be successful you must study success; that *you* are the only key to your better future; that there is no Aladdin's lamp, Tooth Fairy or benevolent Genie who will give you success because you feel you deserve it.

But do you need to compare yourself to the great men and women of our time? Do you need to aim for lofty goals and great deeds? Do you need to become a billionaire entrepreneur before others can say: *"There's a successful person. "*

Frankly, I don't know. And that's because I don't know your specific, Major Life Goal. The success journey needs to be plotted by each individual according to his own aspirations, dreams, needs and wants. If you want to become the Secretary General of the United Nations, that's fine. If that's what you really want, then that's what your friends and family should also want for you.

On the other hand if your aspirations are to nurture a happy family life and provide financial and emotional security for yourself and your family, that's great! If that's what you want, then that's what I want for you too.

The point is that it is up to each of us to write and live our own story line. Let others apply their aspirations to their own life.

What prevents many from living a story line written by themselves is that parents, society and experience have written a storyline *for* them. Success begins when we write our own story line and live it through Self leadership and Personal Excellence.

So if you are going to change *your* life forever, when is the best time to start? When is the right moment?

What about right now?

Let this be the moment you cry; *Enough!* Let this be the moment you commit yourself deeply and wholly to achieving success in all the major spheres of your life.

Then *begin* to live it!

Because the very moment you *actually begin to live* your own storyline will be the very moment you change your life forever.

2

The 'Rule Book'

30 Success Fundamentals

Why were 15,200 of 16,000 American men and women regarded as failures?

In a survey by Napoleon Hill only 5% were regarded as successful. Yet they all had the same government, the same economy, the same language, the same 24 hours per day, the same weather...

Their world too was bursting with opportunities, ready to welcome anyone who could make a better shoe, dig a better hole, invent a cleaner fuel, think a better thought, write a better book, make himself more valuable......

What was the 5% factor that made all the difference?

If the survey were carried out today, in which group would it find you?

Are there fewer opportunities for you now than there were before? If you think so 92% of all scientists who ever walked the Earth would probably disagree with you. How do I know? Because 92% of all scientists who ever lived are alive today! Such is the promise of the future!

Yet only a few people see gold where many see rock and hard work!

What are the secrets of success that make the difference between triumph and defeat; wealth and poverty; success and failure?

Is there a 'book of rules' for success? A set of laws enabling all to succeed to their fullest potential?

In ancient Greece they got it down to seven 'Pillars of Wisdom':

1.   Know Thyself - Euclid

2.   Look to the End of Life - Chilo

3.   Seize Occasion - Pittacus

4.   The Mean is Best - Cleobulus

5.   The Most of Men Are Evil - Bias

6.   In Industry is All - Periander

7.   Haste, if Thou Woulds't Fail - Thales

Study of success experiences from 500BC to the present era establishes one overriding truth; there is no secret for achieving success without having to work for success. Nature's Law of Growth forbids it.

However there are laws which have been known for millennia. Yet rather than study and apply them, many people choose to suffer the misery of want; to accept; to adjust; to surrender their life to circumstances; to live by default rather than by design.

Thomas J Watson, founder of I.B.M., tried to help his employees succeed by inspiring them to; *think, observe, discuss, listen.*

He had these injunctions printed on the steps of the I.B.M. office so they would be seen every day. All these are qualities of Self leadership.

To design the life you want to live rather than live a life written for you by others is a prerequisite for wholistic success. Know the success fundamentals which, taken as a whole, could be said to form a 'book of rules'. Eventually you will want to form your own 'book of rules' which might include some or all the rules shown here. That will be a great moment for you. It will mark the moment when you will have truly arrived as a strong leader of self.

Susan Mitchell, Australian author of 'Tall Poppies' and 'Tall Poppies Too', says of the women leaders she has studied; *"What really unites them is a common framework for viewing themselves and the world.*

The following book of success 'rules' provides a framework for anyone embarked on a personal success journey. You don't have to *like* the rules. But you would be wise to know them.

Know the Formula for Success

At the end of your working life will you be content to say;

"I didn't succeed because I didn't have the formula?"

So you will never have to say you didn't have the formula for Wholistic Success, here it is:

$$\frac{S = Asl^2}{PE}$$ Success = Attitude times Self-leadership
    Squared over Personal Excellence

The emphasis is on the power of Self leadership; on doing things.

Success does not depend on our ability to follow or lead others, but on our ability to lead ourselves.

This first fundamental is the most profound key to unlocking our mind and opening it to self-discovery, personal excellence and lifelong success.

The ability to lead ourselves means having the ability to self-discipline, to self-reward. It takes us out of the passenger seat and places us right behind the steering wheel.

Through the perspective of Self leadership a whole new world opens to us. We needn't wait to be prodded or cajoled; forced or threatened. We take our own lead. We manage our own day to day business. We accept the responsibility for setting and achieving our own goals.

The biggest challenge of success is more than running our own business; more than earning independence and wealth. It is a challenge for us to accept responsibility for our own life and, having done so, fulfill the promise of our future.

The other major determinant for attaining Wholistic Success is *Personal Excellence.* Without this quality you might *accomplish* (i.e. obtain wealth) but what is the good of wealth without health and happiness?

You might find *Self leadership* a difficult part of the equation. This is not surprising because it demands organization, energy, application, courage, working to a specific Major Life Goal.

If you love what you do, deeply believe in what you do and are wholly committed to it, Self leadership will be a pleasure, not a task.

Determine your Specific Major Life Goal

Do you remember your teens when the world was a place to conquer? There were dreams to fulfill. Energy was boundless. Nothing was impossible. You were going to live forever!

Given the same feelings and the knowledge that you couldn't fail; what *could* you be? Forget difficulty. Forget present restraints. Let your mind soar; what *could* you be?

What happened to the dream? To the teenager who was full of hope for the future? What were the detours?

Are you doing what you want to do? If income were not a consideration, what would you be doing instead? What *could* you be?

The Australian biographer of 'Montgomery', Alan Moorehead, refused to continue along a detour from his Major Life Goal.

Early in life he decided to become a writer. However he felt pressured to study law and even paid for his University education by selling free-lance stories.

Realising that becoming a lawyer was a detour he decided not to sit for his final exam; making that decision the day before it. Instead he took up a post as a journalist to develop his writing skills and achieved his goal.

People who know what they want achieve it despite the story line others might have written for them.

Michelangelo's father beat him because he wanted to be a sculptor and painter. World famous playwright Henrick Ibsen was intended to be a chemist; Isaac Newton was meant to be a farmer; Rubens was meant to be a lawyer; Nikola Tesla and Charles Darwin were meant to be priests .... and so the list goes on... and on.

Find a dream. What *could* you be? Write a clear, concise statement of your mission in life. Write it down! Know what you want, when you want it, why you want it, how you plan to achieve it and what you are prepared to do (discipline) to get it.

If you don't have a specific Major Life Goal you'll be part of someone else's plan for theirs. Can you guess how much someone else has planned for you?

Determine Areas in Which You Want Success

We have already seen that to be attained, success must be defined. As we live many 'lives' it is important to define the success you want in your:

- Personal Life

- Family Life

- Community Life

- Business/Work Life

- Financial Life

- Spiritual Life

One broad definition will not serve because each sphere is unlike any other sphere.

Define What Success Means For You

Defining success is not as simple as it might appear to someone whose concept of it is limited to money.

To some, success can mean freedom from mortgages, from debts; freedom to buy what they need whenever they need it; freedom to help others; to change jobs.

The great **H.G. Wells** held that;

"Wealth, notoriety, place or power are no measure of success whatever. The only true measure of success is the ratio between what one might have been and done on one hand, and the thing we have made and made of ourselves on the other."

To Mother Teresa success might mean living a life of service to the poor and needy.

How would you define success? If you don't have a clear idea of what it is, how will you know when you have it? How will you know to achieve it?

In forming our personal definition of success we need to acknowledge that success is not a future event, nor is it a destination.

The Wholistic view is that Success is in the Life as it is lived.

For example, what is the point of accumulating wealth to age 65, retiring and virtually waiting for ...... what?

The Wholistic philosophy maintains that success is a dynamic of life. It must be, or we would still be living in trees.

Success grows with each achievement throughout life. It does not simply fall into place at some single, distant point.

You are living success to your individual extent right now. By wanting 'success' you probably mean that you want to increase the level of success you have already.

Understand the Law of Growth

A property of growth is sequence. For example; you must be a baby before you can be a child; you must be a child before you can be an adult.

The law of growth affects all living things. It also affects our *understanding* and provides us with knowledge, experience and maturity of judgement.

Can total knowledge be acquired in an instant? If a person were kept in a totally dark room for years and the blind were suddenly lifted, would not the sunlight daze him? Is it not more effective to lift the blind little by little so he can absorb the light gradually?

We all grow at different rates. We need to 'fail' several times before we begin to succeed (as in learning to walk). We grow through trial, error, success. We acquire knowledge through experience and study; all of which takes time.

As success is a process of living, some people will succeed more quickly than will others. It is nonsense to be crestfallen over the fact that at 30 years of age you might not have achieved the success you want. The law of growth affects everyone differently.

Measure success growth against the progress you have made since your last measure; not against someone else.

Accept the Law of Change

To Life's certainties of death and taxes we could add change as another sure bet.

Did you ever consider the many bodies in which you have lived? You lived in a seven year old body; a teenager's body; and there is the body in which you live now. Without change you would stay as helpless as at birth.

Change occurs in every sphere of life. Many of the opinions you held as a child might have changed. You change your mind, your clothes, your car, your school, house, etc.

One would think that having practiced and lived through change all our lives, we would respond to new change in a positive manner.

Yet only a minority adapt to and succeed through change. Most people cope and survive while about a third of those affected, go under.

This is quite surprising when you consider that we ask for change when we ask for more success.

The key to succeeding through change, therefore, must lie in how we choose to respond.

The thing to remember is; It's only change.

We can choose to react or respond to it. There is a world of difference. When we go to a doctor we can respond to the treatment and get better, or react to it and get worse.

A formula for dealing with change more successfully is:

- Acknowledge the change

- Accept the change

- Achieve the change

Of course, some change can be disastrous (to health, the environment, etc). However it's important to know the difference between fighting change for a noble cause and resisting it because it will prize you out of your comfort zone.

Progress would be wonderful if it would stop!

Put in That Extra Effort

The reward for making that extra effort is opportunity.

Decide how hard you should work; 8 hours per day five days per week? Six days per week? 12 Hours per day? You need to decide for yourself. This decision will form a vital part of your personal success philosophy.

Kemmons Wilson, the founder of Holiday Inns - never graduated from High School. Addressing students at a graduation ceremony he said;

"I really don't know why I'm here. I never got a degree, and I've only worked half days my entire life. I guess my advice to you is to do the same. Work half days every day. And it doesn't matter which half ..... the first 12 hours or the second 12 hours."

Over 75% of millionaires in the United States of America are people who have worked 6 to 7 days per week, up to 10-12 hours per day for 20-30 years.

It is the effort they have been willing to make for financial success.

Arguably the world's most versatile genius, Leonardo Da Vinci had it all worked out centuries ago with this prayer;

"O Lord, You give us everything for the price of effort."

The famous French Artist Tolouse Lautrec insisted on supervising every phase of printing his works. After a night out he would sleep in a cab outside the print shop waiting for it to open so he could be on hand to ensure the work was done to his satisfaction.

That's extra effort!

Use Nature's Law of Increasing Returns

Sow one grain of wheat and it brings forth a bushel; sow one apple seed and it produces an orchard.

That's how life works.

The law of increasing returns applies to negative as well as to positive sowing. If you are the type who lives in the past, resists change, hands out bad news or pukes your problems onto others, your negativity will come back to you a hundredfold.

Negative sowers are morale saboteurs. Over time others lose respect for them, enjoy themselves more and are happier when they're not around.

With whom are you associating? What are you letting them do to you? What are you becoming? Associate with people who have high expectations. (Have you ever seen a statue to a critic?)

Sow positive thoughts and feelings so you harvest a bounty of respect, recognition, achievement and reward. Do it with enthusiasm, cheerfulness and a positive mental attitude.

Apply Self Leadership

E.M. Gray spent most of his life looking for the one denominator common to all successful people. To paraphrase what he said; 'The successful person has the habit of doing things failures don't like to do, of leading themselves to do them.'

All great leaders are great self-leaders.

Successful people might not like to do everything they have to do, but their dislike is subordinated to their strength of purpose.

Self leadership includes adherence to a set of values and code of behaviour. It is also thought control; emotion control, laziness control.

There is excitement in the ability to make ourselves do things, especially those things we thought we could never do.

Many well known people had to learn to lead themselves to do things before they could become successful. One method which has worked well for them is to set a daily goal.

Author W. Somerset Maugham declared:

"Wherever I've gone and whatever I've done I have kept in mind that each day I must write from 1,000 to 1,500 words."

Emile Zola's motto for Self leadership was *"Not a day without a line"*.

Scientist Sir Thomas Huxley believed that;

"Duty is to the thing we ought to do, at the time we ought to do it, whether we feel like doing it or not".

Famous composer Giacomo Rossini had himself locked in for three days so he made himself write the opera 'Othello'.

Tchaikovsky said;

"One cannot afford to sit waiting for inspiration; she is a guest that does not visit the lazy, but comes only to those who call her. Very often one must first conquer laziness and lack of inclination."

Even talent needs strong Self leadership to learn how it can be used. Famed tenor Luciano Pavarotti told Dr Germaine Greer that it takes him three years to learn a role. He vocalizes throughout the day before a performance.

Self leadership gets us moving whether we feel like it or not.

How can you learn if you can't lead yourself? How can you persist? How can you be single-minded in achieving your goals?

If you can't lead yourself you'll be led by others.

Ray Kroc, founder of the MacDonald's Corporation, says;

"The essential factor that lifts one man above his fellows in terms of achievement and success is his capacity for greater self-discipline."

Success depends on your ability to master and apply daily Self leadership.

Develop a Pleasing Personality

Studies in the U.S. suggest that 10 seconds is all it takes to form a first opinion of someone new. 55% of this opinion is based on what we wear; 37% on body language and attitude, and only 7% on what we actually say.

Our character, the clothes we wear, our facial expressions, the way we smile, shake hands; all help create an impression.

If people like you they'll be more likely to help you.

There must be hundreds of thousands of people who have little or no idea what is in their insurance policies. They bought the salesperson's personality as much as anything else.

A pleasing personality is the key to rapport. Taking a 'human interest' in other people's welfare is its cornerstone.

Buddha's view was that 'To conquer oneself is a greater task than conquering others'.

Apply Clear, Accurate Thinking

Not that long ago people believed steel ships couldn't float; that only birds could fly; that if a train sped at 20 mph passengers would suffocate; that London would be made impassable by 'mountains' of horse droppings.

Other examples of unclear thinking are:

- Blaming others or circumstances for our own shortcomings (excusitis)

- Waiting for others to lead us instead of leading ourselves

- Wishing things were easier, instead of making ourselves better

- Wanting fewer challenges instead of developing more skills to handle them

- Wanting to be a millionaire; without first becoming a thousandaire; a hundredthousandaire etc.

- Saying things cost too much, instead of admitting we can't afford them.

Clear, accurate thinking is vital to success.

Here are some tips:

- Learn to separate facts from information

- Deal only with relevant facts.

- Don't exaggerate or over-react.

- Don't act on gossip.

- Look for evidence before drawing conclusions.

- Question everything, including your own assumptions.

Concentrate Your Effort and Thought

Life is full of side roads and detours. They can take the form of job offers with more pay. If you don't concentrate your effort towards your Major Life Goal you could easily fall for the temptation of a job that leads away from your goal; a detour with more pay, but a detour!

Charles Goodyear worked for ten years to find a way of vulcanizing rubber. Despite poverty and hardship he refused to take any detours.

Napoleon Bonaparte said;

"When you have an enterprise on hand concentrate upon it wholly; forget that anything else in the world exists".

Learn to focus your mind on the issues at hand until you decide on a definite course.

Make thought concentration a habit. You'll develop an increased ability to solve problems; see weaknesses in arguments and possibly save thousands of dollars by avoiding errors.

Years ago Russell Conwell made six million dollars from one lecture; 'Acres of Diamonds'. On concentration he says;

"Whatever you have to do at all, put your whole mind into it and hold it there until that is all done. This principle can be adopted by nearly all ..... This principle makes men great almost anywhere"

Develop Co-operation and Synergy

Co-Operation makes organised effort possible and creates synergy; that unique phenomenon where $2 + 2$ can equal 8, or 50, or 100! Synergy is where the total of the whole is greater than the sum of its parts.

You have probably experienced it many times; perhaps at a meeting or in a field trip where you had to surmount an obstacle. Everyone contributed and came up with a better solution than any individual could have found.

In his life study of success Napoleon Hill struggled to identify this phenomenon. He called it 'The Master Mind Alliance' and gave it an almost spiritual quality.

He found that when people gather in a spirit of harmony to solve a problem for the common good, a 'Master Mind' formed, greater than the sum of each individual mind.

The truth is that to succeed we need the co-operation of other people. Synergy is the result of the willing co-operation of people gathered in a spirit of harmony to achieve a common good.

There has to be something in it for everyone, even at work. Without co-operation work could be transformed into chaos through Malicious Obedience. This happens when staff do not use their judgement in how they apply instructions. They interpret everything literally then say; "That's what you told me to do."

Genuine interest in people's welfare and a sympathetic appreciation of their viewpoint helps greatly to win co-operation.

Know You Can't Fail

There is no such thing as failure, only outcome. We gain from every experience and grow stronger and wiser from every defeat.

Henry Ford said; *"Failure is the chance to start again more intelligently."*

Many people are so afraid of failure they never get started. Yet Thomas Edison 'failed' over 10,000 times before he was able to make his new invention, the gramophone, play the words; "Mary had a little lamb." His reply was;

"I didn't fail 9,999 times. I discovered 9,999 ways it wouldn't work."

Sir Henry Parkes 'failed' many times. He was bankrupted three times; having to sell his tools as an ivory turner to buy food.

He emigrated from England to Australia where he worked as a labourer and generally proved to be totally inept in business. Yet he became an accomplished politician, the Premier of New South Wales and father of Australian Federation.

Famed author, Leon Uris, failed his English examination three times.

Abraham Lincoln was thought a failure when he entered the Black Hawk war as a captain, but came out a private.

No one is a failure. Everyone succeeds to some extent. For example you might earn $35,000 per year. You have been successful to the extent of $35,000 per year. However what you might want is to increase the extent of your success to earn more.

It is pointless determining success by comparison with others because there will always be someone more and less successful than yourself. It is far better to measure your success against your own previous successes. For example, by earning more this year than last year you have increased your success in the financial sphere of your life.

Napoleon Hill discovered there are few, if any, successful people on Earth who have not 'failed' many times before they began to succeed.

Setbacks merely defer success. We have to be around when that later time comes. We can't be there if we quit.

Be Tolerant of Others

Time shows that much of what we hold true is false, based on incomplete knowledge or on misunderstanding.

An extreme case of intolerance is found in the saga of Australian explorer Robert O'Hara Burke. Dying of starvation as he proceeded along the bed of Cooper's Creek towards Mount Hopeless, he refused food from friendly Aborigines because he regarded them as "Below his station!" Consequently he and a fellow explorer; William John Wills, perished. Their companion, a more sensible man named King, accepted the food and survived.

Dr Samuel Johnson said;

"If God Himself does not propose to judge man until the end of his days, how can I?"

Show a Humane Regard For People

Andrew Carnegie was a great humanitarian. After his death a note stating his Major Life Goal was found taped inside his desk drawer. His goal was to spend half his life accumulating wealth and the other half in giving it away.

Ask yourself;

"How will my actions in achieving my Major Life Goal create a win-win situation for myself and others?"

You might remember the story of a man who wanted money so much he betrayed his best friend to get it.

What he had become could not be erased by money. He lost his self-respect. Instead of happiness his treasure brought misery and despair.

He tried to return the money, but those who paid him said;

"You got what you wanted and we got what we wanted. So keep your money".

He threw the money away but it was too late. What he had become in acquiring his treasure had destroyed his self.

Within a few days he hanged himself from a tree.

His name was Judas Iscariot.

Wholistic success means achieving our goal without compromising Personal Excellence (integrity, honour, self-respect), without causing harm to others. How can we achieve this unless our goal is obtained in a way which serves others honestly and creates opportunities also for them?

Think and Apply a Win-Win Philosophy

In the words of Stephen R. Covey;

"Win/Win is not a technique, it is a total philosophy of human interaction. To win doesn't have to mean "to beat".

If others don't win when we do, what sort of community will we create? Here's a glimpse:

In Rio de Janeiro wealthy citizens barricade themselves behind high walls - some employ armed guards - to protect themselves from their own community. Is that success?

In Bophal the environment is so polluted that life expectancy is drastically cut and community health has been described as a disaster. Why? Because some locally based multi-nationals strive for dollar success despite the enormous damage they inflict on the world - and people - around them.

Is that success?

Personally we might not be able to do very much for Rio or Bophal, but we can embrace a win/win philosophy in our Totem (code by which to live.)

Manage Time Effectively

We've all met people who keep saying; *"If only I had more time!"* Regardless what we do, beg, steal or borrow, 24 hours a day is all we are entitled to and all we get. So doesn't it make sense to manage it?

We are paid for the results we achieve with time. The more value time we put in, the higher our income. If we want more income, we must become more valuable.

When you get your next 24 hour ration, how much of it will you convert to *value* time? How much of it will you control? How much of it will control you?

Put Quality In, Get Quality Out

Your mind is a vast, wonderful library. It stores information you and others put into it. It employs a faithful 'librarian'.

When you want to recall a fact or feeling your librarian will sift through all the data you've collected to make it available to you.

However faithful and efficient your librarian might be, it can only retrieve what you have collected.

In other words, if you put quality in, your 'librarian' will get quality out!

Consider the T.V. you watch and the books you read. Ask yourself; *"Is this information I am storing in my mental library positive or negative? Will it help me achieve wealth, health and happiness?"*

Remember, you can only get quality out if you put quality in.

Grow Through Effort

Knowledge, when organised and applied is the fuel which powers our modern world. Success or the lack of it results from the choices we make based on the knowledge we have.

To apply knowledge takes Self leadership, effort, energy and determination. Simply knowing how to be successful will not make you so unless you lead yourself to achieve it.

How many people do you know who have a wooden leg? (A ready excuse for not trying) They are either too old, too ill, too unschooled, don't know how....etc. They might have excusitis, the affliction of low-achievers.

Here are some people who turned their back on excusitis listed under the most common forms of excuse:

Excuse: Too Old

Konrad Adenauer was Chancellor of West Germany. Under his leadership West Germany became an economic giant, rebuilt its defence force and provided a cornerstone for European unity. He began his 14 year term of office at the age of 73.

Dr Dennis Wheatley, sports psychologist, author, motivator and speaker admitted he didn't get started until he was 45. Abraham Lincoln didn't begin to succeed in the Presidential stakes until he was over 50. J.P. Morgan - the power in world finance - made his vast fortune after 60.

Miguel De Cervantes, author of 'Don Quixote' didn't do anything of any substance until after he was 48. Leonardo Da Vinci was over 60 when he painted the Mona Lisa. P.T. Barnum, the great circus owner and showman, didn't start his circus until he was over 60. President Woodrow Wilson was still a college professor at 50. Aristotle, one of the world's great philosophers, started his work at 50.

Excuse: Too Ill

Chopin suffered from severe lung disease. Despite his illness which amounted to a slow death, he wrote preludes, fantasies, waltzes and ballads that have enriched the world.

Frederick Schiller, a consummate poet, was devastated by illness when aged 30. He was in constant pain, weak and breathed with difficulty because one lung was stuck to his chest wall, yet he worked fourteen hours each day on happy hymns and beautiful poetry.

Julius Caesar, William of Orange, William Van Loon (painter), William Pitt (British Prime Minister), James Watt, Sir Walter Scott - all were debilitated by constant, severe headaches. Countless others also achieved greatness by writing their own storyline despite personal suffering; others such as poet Alexander Pope, composer Sir Arthur Sullivan, writers Eugene O'Neill, Robert Louis Stevensen and Helen Keller.

Excuse: No Place to Work

Johan Strauss wrote waltzes while eating at a restaurant. Harriet Beecher Stowe, author of Uncle Tom's Cabin, wrote whilst working in her kitchen.

Founder of the Methodist Church and charismatic preacher John Wesley wrote his sermons as he was walking. Marie Curie used a store room in a basement for her early experiments on uranimum. The father of bacteriology and Nobel Prize winner Robert Koch carried out experiments on his front porch because he had no room in his house.

Charles Goodyear experimented with vulcanising rubber while in prison for being unable to pay his debts. Marco Polo wrote his 'Travels' whilst in prison.

Giorgio Vassari reminds us:

"No Man distinguishes himself in any art who is not ready to beat the cold, heat, hunger and thirst. He who imagines that he can become great by taking his ease in pleasant surroundings is much mistaken."

Apparently Dr Henry Wieman didn't agree with him:

"Wishing to improve his intellectual life, he procured a large, comfortable chair, slippers and cosy jacket. A bookrest was attached to his chair to hold the book under a special reading lamp at the correct angle before his eyes. A revolving bookcase stood alongside. He equipped himself with pens, paper and eyeshade. After the evening meal he would come into the study, put on his jacket and slippers, adjust the lamp and place the book on its rest. When everything was arranged, he would recline in the chair with eyeshade over his eyes and.......... go to sleep!"

(From 'Spare a Minute!' by Howard Crago)

Excuse: Too Broke

The woman who built one of the world's great business houses, Coco Chanel, was raised in poverty. So were Pierre Cardin and Rudolph Nureyev.

Famous author and humanist Emile Zola lived mostly on sparrows which he caught and roasted on the end of a curtain rod. Vincent Van Gogh, Mozart, George Washington Carver, Andrew Carnegie and countless others achieved the life they designed for themselves despite the fact that initially they were broke.

One of America's great businessmen, founder of IBM Thomas J. Watson

"Was once reduced to sleeping on a pile of sponges in the basement of a drugstore. He had only one suit to his name,

*and when he could afford to get it pressed he had to wait in
the back of the tailor shop in his underwear until it was ready. "*
(He rose to become the highest paid man in America.)

(From 'Father, Son and Co.')

Excuse: Not Educated

Neither were the great bulk of the world's achievers. Schooling
might get you a job, but self-education can make you rich!

The fact you are studying now shows you are doing something
about your self-education. You have joined the famous company of Jesus, Thomas Jefferson, Benjamin Franklin, Edison,
Henry Ford and many thousands of others who didn't have
enough 'education'. They taught themselves because they were
self-leaders.

In the end excusitis is a 'wooden leg'; a reason to excuse lack
of effort.

Every day in many ways 'ordinary' men and women are turning
their backs to excusitis. All it takes is a specific Major Life
Goal built on Personal excellence, a determination to succeed,
a blueprint for achieving the life you want, heartfelt commitment to take the steps that will change your life forever and the
self-leadership to get it done.

See Difficulties as Opportunities

In 1979 the Arab oil exporters initiated a world economic crisis
through massive increases in the price of crude oil. Among the
countries worst affected was Japan, who imported 85% of its
oil from the Middle East.

Overnight, there was panic. Japan's trading position worsened
instantly and it seemed that it could devastate its economy.

The government took immediate steps. It launched a nation-
wide economy drive to reduce its use of energy. It restructured
its economy and replaced old technology with new, energy-ef-
ficient and productive equipment. It launched whole-heartedly

into automation and became first to use industrial robots to build cars.

The result? Japan converted enormous difficulty into great opportunity. The economy's restructure and automation transformed Japan into an economic superpower.

So complete was Japan's success that when a similar price hike was inflicted on the world some years later, its economy hardly missed a beat.

The crisis was only opportunity dressed as difficulty.

Josiah Wedgewood experienced great difficulty. As a result of his limp (which later led to amputation) he could no longer turn the potter's wheel so he experimented with vases, plates, cameos and fine quality porcelain. Eventually a statue was erected in his honour, unveiled by Prime Minister William Gladstone who travelled from London to Burslem to honour a 'common potter'.

Opening new doors is not difficult when you have the keys.

Ann Landers said that;

"Opportunities are usually disguised as hard work, so most people don't recognise them".

Opportunity searches for the prepared and moves on when it does not find them.

Popular singer Engelbert Humperdinck's opportunity to achieve stardom came when Alec Fyne, Head of Light Entertainment Casting at ATV phoned Lew Grade to say their star for that night's episode of 'Sunday Night at the London Palladium' had missed his plane. Alec suggested a relatively unknown, Engelbert Humperdinck.

The rest is history.

What would have happened if Engelbert had said; *"I'm not ready"*?

The great tenor Luciano Pavarotti drew a London crowd of 100,000 including prime ministers and princes who stood in pouring rain for over two hours to hear him sing.

How did Luciano get his opportunity? Again, at the London Palladium the opera star Giuseppe di Stefano could not appear because of illness. Luciano Pavarotti was at the beginning of his career and had spent years in preparation.

What would have happened to that opportunity if he had said, "Give me a few years to prepare!"

Do not be surprised if highly paid jobs or opportunities are more difficult to execute successfully. It has been so for past generations and will be so for your generation too.

By preparing you will develop the skill to convert difficulties into opportunities; opportunities into successes; successes into achievement of your specific Major Life Goal.

Exercise *possibility* thinking.

Prevent Erosion of Achievement

The overall aim of wholistic success is to achieve, through Self Leadership and Personal Excellence, wealth, health and happiness, to keep it and to enrich your community through it.

However everything in life is subject to erosion. Through decisions we do or do not make we can lose or diminish the success we have.

Success requires maintenance. We need to mend our fences; live off our interest not our capital; increase our knowledge and acquire new ideas; manage expenses; watch cash receipts; attend to daily Self leadership; weigh, measure, count and be prepared for tough times. Success is rarely a case of 'have arrived; sit back and enjoy gourmet living'. It happens a day at a time, growing as we grow, living as we live. It is a dynamic of life. Life itself is the product of a string of biological successes. Yet is it not subject to quick death and decay if unattended?

Accept That You Are the Only One Who Can Succeed For You

Jim MacDonald, award-winning Sales Manager for one of the largest insurance companies in Australia says;

"Walk into any book shop and you will see many titles which include the word 'Secret' - The Secret to Success, Happiness, Money, Marriage, Sex, Health, Fitness, Sport and so on.

"If, like me, you have eagerly purchased one or more of these books in the hope that your wishes will be fulfilled, your dreams realized, then like me, I'm sure you will have known disappointment. At the ripe 'young age' of 49, I am convinced that the 'real' secret is that there is no secret - no easy way, no short cut which will guarantee 'success'.

"Rather there are a range of views, ideas, experiences, teachings, lessons, methods and systems which have worked well for others and which are deserving of trial to find what works for you."

The familiar saying; "If it is to be, it is up to me" speaks volumes.

To obtain wholistic success we need to pursue its three elements simultaneously. We can't say; *"I'll become rich first and worry about happiness later".*

History has bleached the bones of those who tried that approach. They become wealthy but bereft of true friends and any hope of real happiness. These people might be rich (an accomplishment) but are not wholistically successful.

John Kenneth Galbraith said;

"I am not quite sure what the advantage is in having a few more dollars to spend if the air is too dirty to breathe, the water too polluted to drink, the commuters are losing out in the struggle to get in and out of the city, the streets are filthy, and the schools so bad that the young perhaps wisely stay away, and the hoodlums roll citizens for some of the dollars they saved in the tax cut".

Be Prepared for Success

Time. Effort. Maintaining a positive mental attitude. Study. Avoiding negativity. Practicing daily Self leadership. Persistence. Steadily moving towards your Major Life Goal. That is what is meant by preparation.

That is not a price you have to pay. You pay the price of failure, not of success.

Success brings benefits, not bills.

Too many people are content to pay the price of failure. They want success but are slaves to routine. They wait on the dock for their 'ship to come in', but don't send any ships out.

They go to work, come home, eat, watch T.V. and go to sleep. They do this five or more days a week year in, year out.

Most people spend so much time watching television they could earn a fortune.

Successful people do what unsuccessful people won't do!

What if people cut their T.V. time in half and used the time saved to study wealth, health and happiness?

Could their outlook change?

Could that change lead to a better life? A life based on Personal Excellence?

With a new sense of direction could they become wealthier? Happier?

Have Specific Reasons for Wanting Success

Why do you want success? List your *specific* reasons. Write them down. Make sure they are good enough to motivate you; to inspire you to act; to change your life forever.

For some people philanthropy is their chief reason for striving to succeed.

Others want to succeed to provide a comfortable, secure life for themselves and for those they love.

Yet others want success because of their strong disgust; their frustration with their life; with having to beg for every small pay increase; with having to go without things they need; with saying "No" to their children because they can't afford what they want. They are disgusted and frustrated with living in the shadow of debt and worry.

By listing your specific reasons for wanting success in your 'Positive Self-Awareness' file you'll stay true to yourself. You will motivate your spirit every time you read them. You will be in less danger of losing your sense of self, of forgetting where you want to be and why you want to be there.

Think and See Yourself How You Want to Be

The discipline of psycho-cybernetics is built upon the maxim: 'We become how we think and see ourselves to be.'

The human race has known about this great truth for thousands of years! Yet how many have read such phrases over and over without giving them more than a few seconds of thought?

Visualisation of success achievement is not new.

In the battle of Zama in 202bc the Roman general Scipio defeated Hannibal and saved Rome. Before the battle he inspired his legionnaires by reminding them of their recent successes in Africa. He asked them to visualise the success which surely would be theirs.

The way it works is this; think and believe success and you'll be successful; think and believe failure and you will surely fail. This also applies to how you see yourself as a human being.

Zig Ziglar tells the story of a boy who was born to an unwed mother in times when that stigma could be unbearable.

Women would whisper within earshot "Do they know who the father is?" Some of them would not let their children play with a 'bastard son'. The boy and his mother were ostracised.

He felt an outcast; valueless and rejected. He avoided mixing with people and withdrew into himself. Until one day, something happened that changed his life.

One Sunday just as the church service ended and the boy was about to leave, the minister stepped down from the pulpit and with a loud booming voice asked him; "And whose child are you?"

Everyone held their breath.

The minister walked up, looked him in the eye and said;

"I know whose child you are! The family resemblance is unmistakable! You are a child of God! That's quite a heritage you have there, boy! Now see you live up to it!"

Eventually that boy became governor. His self perception as someone rejected and valueless had changed to that of someone special.

The person who ultimately becomes successful is the one who believes he can!!

How?

The nervous system does not distinguish between a real or imagined experience. It files both stimuli into our mental library.

It has much to do with the godlike human quality; imagination.

Our imagination can take us to the vast reaches of the universe; create poignant musical phrases; capture a soul on canvas; lift our hearts with sweetest poetry; build great nations.

Dr Charles Garfield studied peak performers in NASA, business and sport. He found that peak performers are visualisers. They imagine and see the success they will achieve.

Sports psychologists in the USA carried out an interesting imagination exercise involving two basketball teams. They asked one team to carry on with their physical training.

They asked the second team to train only with their imagination. Guess which team won? You're right! The team that trained only with their imagination won.

Be Happy

We become happy from the moment we decide to feel and act happy, just as we begin to succeed from the moment we decide to be successful.

In the book; 'Tall Poppies Too' by Susan Mitchell, Carmel Niland says;

"Happiness comes from knowing that what you are is not dependent on titles, or degrees, or job descriptions. It's not dependent on anything other than your intrinsic worth, which is incalculable."

Unhappiness is ugly; a cancer of the spirit. We can't wait for others or other things to make us happy. (What are you going to be in the meantime?)

Think success and happiness! Believe success and happiness! Imagine success and happiness!

If you have a Major Life Goal built on Personal Excellence and value to the community it can help you achieve happiness through the power of purpose.

If as you have thought and believed, therefore you are, it follows that as you think and believe from now on, so you will be.

Use It or Lose It

The power to imagine; to love; to think clearly; positively; these and many others need constant use. If you don't use them, you'll lose them.

The principle can be demonstrated quite dramatically.

Australian Rod Laver is one of the world's great tennis champions. As a boy he had a weak left arm. To strengthen it he kept a squash ball in his left pocket and squeezed it almost continuously. Eventually his left arm grew almost twice as large as his right. The law of use worked. He won the Wimbledon Crown four times and in the process became the world's first tennis millionaire.

Does a musician retain and develop his talent by playing constantly, or by not playing at all?

Do you become a better chess player, logician, problem solver, etc., by applying your mind often, or seldom?

Yet millions of people are content to hand over their mind to a television for 40 hours each week! Think of it! They put as much time into watching T.V. as they do into their job!

There is much to be gained by watching T.V. selectively. Simply apply the rule of 'quality in - quality out' to filter programmes that take your mind for an aimless stroll or put it into 'Park'.

You can't develop your mind's full potential by constantly handing it over to a box which tells you what to think and when to laugh! Like any other organ, the brain must be used if it is to remain useful.

As psychologist Dr Susan Jeffers maintains;

"I know of no one who has been able to make 'permanent' a positive way of thinking without practice. Such people may exist, I simply haven't met them. In my experience, if you don't practice, you lose the skill. This is the point most people don't seem to understand."

(From 'Feel the Fear and Do It Anyway')

Practice and use your success skills and your boss might begin to see you as promotion material. Your colleagues could develop a new respect for the way you throw yourself into your job; for your cheerfulness; your encouraging words; your willingness to share with and help other people, for your Self leadership and Personal Excellence.

Anticipate and Prepare for the Tough Times

There's nothing new about tough times. Those always come and go.

The key is to accept that most of the time, life is difficult. Either there is a problem at work, at home, with your neighbour etc. When you accept that life is difficult, then you can proceed to make it better through Self leadership.

The common alternative is to develop the 'Martyr Complex' (everything happens to me) and look for 'social aspirins' such as alcohol. But that doesn't make tough times any better.

Even for members of 'The Lucky Sperm Club' (born into wealth) life can be difficult.

It is not the tough times that defeat us. It is the way we see them and what we do - or don't do - about them that decides the outcome.

Tough times are opportunities for us to become stronger; wiser; better, more understanding and compassionate; more humane.

They force us to challenge our self perception, our resourcefulness, our motives, our ties with others, our values, our personal Totem.

Anyone can sail on calm waters but it takes skill to sail on a stormy sea. Learn to anticipate the storms and prepare for them. Well managed companies do this by keeping a contingency plan. They project ahead 5, 10 even 20 years or more. They also keep reserves. Governments also keep reserves for natural disasters.

Prudent investors protect themselves against risk by spreading their investments over a wide range of portfolios.

The principle of anticipating tough times and preparing for them was demonstrated thousands of years ago on the Yang-Tze River in China.

The river was notorious for its danger to shipping and exacted a heavy toll on the precious cargo of rice. The capsizing of any boat meant loss of an entire harvest. Each year it visited ruin on scores of farmers.

One day an enterprising person suggested that farmers transport only ten percent of their harvest in any one boat. That way if a boat sank only a small part of their crop would be lost.

How can you prepare?

By study; by concentrating on your specific Major Life Goal; by interpreting the world's challenges through your Personal Totem; by working at happy, supportive, personal relationships; by persistence; by anticipation; by daily Self leadership; by not running down your reserves.

Save and Invest

If cash reserves are essential for a well-managed business, then what about for you and me? Businesses exist to produce and share wealth. You are 'You incorporated'. Your 'stock' is your ability to earn an income: Your duty is to develop that ability.

The following could be a sobering exercise. Please answer the questions honestly:

How long have you worked? ________years

In all that time approximately how much have your earned after tax? $________

How much have you saved and invested? (i.e. how much money is in your bank account or in assets?) $________

How much would you have now if you had saved and invested only 10% of all . your earnings? $________

What happened?

When we have saved money it is easier for us to borrow more. It gives us the opportunity to begin a business venture; expand an existing business; increase our capital through investment. It also demonstrates a strong discipline and an ability to repay borrowings. Banks will love us! And so will we.

The alternative is to get into debt for a refrigerator! But non-income producing debt is slavery! It steals our freedom! We are 'owned' by money lenders.

As mentioned earlier, preparing for the 'tough times' requires, among other things, a reserve fund. How can we create this fund and enjoy the peace of mind it brings without regular saving and investment? *(A sage advice is to live on 80% of your income and save and invest the rest.)*

Postscript

For all our learning, struggle and effort, we might not achieve our ultimate goal.

So why try at all?

In the philosophy of wholistic success, the money you make or the goal you attain is only secondary. A more important reason to strive for success is for the person you become in the process.

There are countless stories of people who have made and lost fortunes only to make another soon afterwards. In succeeding the first time they gained the disciplines, knowledge and skill to do it again.

They had become new people.

Even if you do not succeed in your ultimate goal you can succeed part way and live much more successfully than if you had not tried at all!

It's just as easy to try as not to try and you've got to live until you die, so if you don't lead yourself to wholistic success, what else are you going to do with your life?

3

Attitude Barriers

Old battle cries such as; "Have a positive mental attitude" and "It's your attitude, not your aptitude, that determines your altitude" are all very well, but when they are touted as the key to success we have to be extra careful about taking them out of context.

A positive mental attitude (PMA) of itself, will not make you successful. What can be said about PMA is that it will help you do almost anything better than you could have done it had you used a negative mental attitude.

For example, if you decided to start a business selling 'widgets', invested your savings and hung up your shingle, PMA will help only if you had done your research, prepared a business plan and knew where, how and when you planned to achieve you goal.

If you had the wrong plan, PMA would only help you fail more cheerfully - and quickly.

However there is more to Attitude than P.M.A.

When most people talk about attitude they usually mean their own. Yet we are influenced just as much by the attitudes of people with whom we work, live and play. The only defence against the negative influence of others is to ensure our own attitude is on track.

Champion Golfer Greg Norman says;

"Sometimes focusing on the negatives creates more negatives. I've never been a negative individual. Never. Let's say I'm playing my bunker shots poorly. Instead of going out there and practicing my bunker shots hour after hour, I'll go chip or hit my five iron instead, something I can be positive about". (Interview with Time's John Garrity, Nov 91)

Remember the game of 'Wooden Leg?' People with poor attitudes are those who play this game most often. It is their excuse for not trying. After all, "What can you expect from someone with a poor attitude/wooden leg?"

An attitude problem is the entry qualification to 'Low Achievers Inc'. Members elect to join this club of their own will. They may cancel their membership anytime - yet choose not to do so. They despair at living a storyline written by others but will not write the storyline they want to live because their attitude prevents them.

Do not mix with low achievers who live by the law of accident. Their 'stinkin' thinkin' can suffocate you. Mix with goal-driven people whose optimism, high expectations, energy and enthusiasm will invigorate you.

Attitude barriers are built block by block. Following are some of the most common:

Wanting a Free Ride

The latter third of the twentieth century has been dubbed by some as 'The Age of Me'. This is meant to describe a self-centred, acquisitive and selfish philosophy.

Some of the symptoms of this philosophy are an increasing demand for government to provide more and more welfare payments, rebates, free services, and so on.

Absenteeism has almost become a right of employment.

In Western Society generally there is much talk of 'Rights' but comparatively little talk of 'responsibility' and 'duty'.

Is it any wonder, therefore, that so many people want success without effort and Self leadership?

Consider the case of Maurice, an electrician working in a small business. His philosophy was to work eight hours per day and not a minute more.

When the business won large contracts he refused to work overtime despite the employer's offer to pay generous allowances. He was dismissed, but clung to his work ethics.

The result? Maurice is 65 and broke. He lives on an age pension and drives a car which has seen much better days. He cannot afford to replace the car, or the very modest house in which he lives, or anything else, for that matter.

Yet he is the first to blame the government for his misfortunes and to cry out for extra handouts.

Maurice has lived his life refusing to put in 'that extra effort'. He is reaping what he has sown. He is paying the price of failure.

Is Maurice unusual?

If you suggested to a colleague that the best way to promote to a senior position was to work hard, produce quality work, do the best for the employer etc.; what sort of reaction do you think you would get? Even if others agreed with you, would they do it? And if they tried, what would fellow workers say?

In almost any field, success depends in large measure on the effort you are willing to give it; on Self leadership.

If you want success you will need to earn it. You will need to reach out to where it is. No one has invented a way of achieving success without effort. If there is no such thing as a free lunch, there certainly is no such thing as a free ride to success.

Self-Doubt

Self doubt is like driving with one foot on the accellerator and the other foot on the brake.

Do you believe you will be successful? Truly successful in all your spheres of life? If your answer is "Yes", that's a good start, but it's not enough. You must transcend belief; you must know.

Belief implies room for doubt. Once you have written your life blueprint for your personal success, defined your mission statement, adopted a personal Totem centred on integrity and committed yourself to achieving your goal, then you will be able to transcend belief and know. When that happens, doubt vanishes. Here's an example:

The manager of the Buenos Aires Opera House was beside himself with worry because the conductor for that evening's performance of 'Aida' was too ill to perform. He asked members of the orchestra if any of them knew the score sufficiently well to conduct it. While others hesitated, an unknown by the name of Arturo Toscanini volunteered. Thus was born the career of one of the greatest conductors of all time.

Did he have doubts? If he did he banished them to the farthest corner of his mind and did it anyway!

Sydney Myer, the poor Russian immigrant who founded the giant Myer Department Store chain, had the motto; *"When in doubt, move forward"*.

A.D. Sertillanges said;

"One finds one's way by taking it"

Sir Philip Sidney said;

"Either I will find a way or I will make one."

Self-doubt is a reality we all have to face. Those nagging thoughts which tell you "Perhaps you can't do it", are echoes from the past.

They could be echoes from your teacher, "Won't you ever get it right?" or from your parents "You're useless!"

Unfortunately our education system does not place great emphasis on 'success conditioning'. It does not ensure each student is given tasks suited to his ability so that he can succeed one step at a time. If this were done, there would be no need for comments like; "When will you ever learn?" "Dummy" etc. No need to grow with self-doubt and fear of success.

These memories are destroyers of confidence and often surface whenever we face difficult tasks. Recognising our conditioning can help banish self-doubt and leave by the wayside those lessons in mediocrity.

However self-doubt can be used positively if you see it as a signal to reassess the job at hand. But don't be limited by ghosts from the past or thoughts of low achievers in the present.

Convert 'obstacle thinking' into 'possibility thinking'

Before Roger Bannister broke the four minute mile experts openly argued whether such a feat was humanly possible. After the breakthrough, 37 other runners broke the four minute mile too!

Roger Bannister had shown it was possible and so others converted doubt into possibility thinking, and achieved!

Two classic gaffes of obstacle thinking were made by Robert Millikan, Nobel Prize winner in physics (1923) when he said;

"There's no likelihood man can ever tap the power of the atom."

and Charles Duell, the head of the American Patent Office (1889) when, with all the authority of his office, he stated:

"Everything that can be invented, has been invented."

If you have considered your plan carefully, researched it, listened to the experiences of those in that field, can transcend the limits of belief and know you can do it, be a Self leader and go for it! Convert doubt and obstacle thinking into possibility thinking.

Procrastination

This affliction can strike any time. It can lose fortunes. It can cost you your life (i.e. procrastinating on a treatment for illness).

No matter how hard you try, you can't put off today. It comes back every morning right on schedule, laden with the baggage of yesterday's unfinished tasks.

Procrastination is a habit and like most habits it can be broken by replacing a bad with a good; by practicing Self leadership.

Why do so many of us procrastinate? Why do you procrastinate?

The answer given for most procrastination is "I don't feel like doing it right now".

However the sad truth is that laziness is a natural trait of human beings, and even high achievers often develop systems to ensure they keep working and have no time to put things off.

One of the most famous prayers in all history was uttered by St Augustine, a great father of the early Christian Church. He pleaded;

"O Lord, give me continence and chastity. Only not yet."

The great philosopher, Immanuel Kant, twice contemplated marriage. He procrastinated for so long that the first woman married someone else and the second woman left town before he completed his deliberations.

Author William James said;

"Nothing is so fatiguing as the eternal hanging-on of an uncompleted task"

Procrastination is such a common thief of success - and life - that it merits detailed discussion. Specific reasons for procrastination can include:

Unpreparedness

You might procrastinate in painting that wall because you don't have the paint, brushes, ladder etc., and so it all seems too much of a bother.

Likewise you might procrastinate in doing 'that course' because you would have to enrol, pay fees, attend an interview, and so on.

The answer here might be to divide the task into two steps; prepare first, execute second.

Unsure How To Do It

Sometimes we might be given a task which we find daunting. Perhaps we are not confident on how to go about it.

In this case it is easy to postpone making a start for as long as possible.

However the task seldom becomes easier by avoiding it. It usually becomes more difficult because by then we have additional work to do.

The answer could be to divide each task into steps and to do it one step at a time. If you need more knowledge, acquire it! Ask. Read. Discuss. Then proceed.

Lethargy

Feeling tired from over-eating, lack of exercise or unfitness is a great ball and chain for the procrastinator. It's so easy to rationalise by saying "I'm not at my best. I wouldn't do it well just now. I'm too tired to concentrate", etc.

Unhappy Home or Work Environment

It's easy to put things off if you're still smarting from a problem at home or work. You're too busy at being angry or hurt to bother about anything else. You want to regurgitate everything that was said, add some things which weren't but should have been said, and generally relive the experience.

Author Colleen McCullough puts the unhappy work environment in this context;

"The thing is that work ought to be enjoyable just because it's work. You should discipline yourself to enjoy what you do.

"One of the things I notice all the time is that no matter what people do, they want it always to be this, that and the other thing. I try to tell people that no matter what you do for a living, it's 90 percent shit. The most paradisiacal job in the world is still 90 percent shit. You do the 90 percent shit to have the 10 percent gold".

(From 'Tall Poppies Too' by Susan Mitchell)

Problems at work or at home are not new and will arise whenever humans work and live together. However brooding over them seldom helps - and can worsen them.

If only we could live in situation-tight compartments. Thick heavy doors would seal off one situation from another. We could then concentrate only on issues at hand.

A little more tolerance, understanding and co-operation help most unhappy situations. Those three elements represent the effort you might have to make whenever you are faced with a personal dilemma.

You might need to talk to a qualified counsellor. If so, don't let your ego or determination to 'get your own way' cancel your future. In old age it won't be the lost deals which we will regret; but the things we should have said; the time we should have spent with those we love; the things we didn't do.

Procrastinating because of unhappiness is no answer to the problem.

Every time we procrastinate we are relinquishing control of a part of our lives. We are following, not leading.

As M. Tupper puts it;

"It is a very waste of life to be and not to do"

When the Task is Too Big

Imagine having a dinner party for eight people. Everyone enjoyed it. You were a great success. However when the party was over you faced a small mountain of soiled plates, glasses, cutlery, pots, pans, casserole dishes, etc.

If you look at the task overall it feels natural to put off making a start - or at least to be reluctant to start.

Suppose you divided the load into segments (i.e. dishes, then cutlery, then pots, etc). Suddenly you've broken down the 'huge' load into a series of smaller ones and the task does not seem so burdensome.

As Dr Robert Schuller says;

"Inch by inch, anything's a cinch".

Rebellion

Have you ever tried to force someone into a task they didn't want to do?

Were you surprised when they kept putting it off? Procrastination can be a form of passive resistance.

If this sounds like you remember it is often better to do the task straight away and get it off your back (if you have no choice). Otherwise be honest in the first place. Tell those concerned that you do not want to do it.

Self-Talk

The principles and effects of suggestion are well documented. Hypnosis would hardly be possible without it. However what might be lesser known are the effects of self-suggestion.

Self-hypnosis in one form or another is practiced by millions of people. It is based on inducing a concentrated state by self-suggestion.

To a lesser extent we too condition our mind to believe things about ourselves.

Our inner dialogues are almost ceaseless. What we say to ourselves affects our confidence, enthusiasm, self-esteem, happiness and general outlook on life.

When faced with a task we wish to postpone, we invariably open an inner dialogue with the various characters within us. It might go something like this;

Character One: *"I should really do it!"*

Character Two: *"Trouble is, I'm basically lazy."*

Character Three: *"What the hell, let it wait another day."*

There we go again, telling ourselves we are lazy (tired, don't really feel like it, etc) and playing the game of 'wooden leg'.

Positive self-talk keeps us from feeding negative self-images into our subconscious. Use positive self-talk to paint a picture of a more determined, energetic you; of a reputation for getting the job done on time, cheerfully and well.

Fear of Criticism/Failure

This fear comes to the fore whenever we lack confidence in our ability to complete a task successfully. We think we'll get it wrong; that we might make a mistake, that we might fail.

So what??

How else can humans gain the experience to succeed?

The way to avoid mistakes is to avoid doing anything! To quit!

Author Colleen McCullough says;

"...I'm a born battler. I love a challenge. I love opposition. Experience adds up. Nothing in life is ever wasted. If there is a God, I know only one thing about him. He hates a quitter. He'll forgive murder ahead of quitting. Life is a gift meant to be used wisely and well. So you keep on trying to make the best of it. You don't give up, and you don't give in".

(From 'Tall Poppies Too' by Susan Mitchell)

It takes single-mindedness and Self leadership to stick to priorities, just as it takes Self leadership and single-mindedness to achieve your Specific, Major Life Goal.

Tom Hopkins has an excellent definition of procrastination;

"Procrastination is the art of living in your yesterdays, avoiding your todays, and ruining your tomorrows."

(From 'How to Master the Art of Selling')

Developing the habit of 'plunging in' can 'kick-start' our engine much faster than could an eternity of thinking about it.

When Sir Walter Raleigh was asked how he got so many things done, he replied;

"When there is anything to do, I start it"

Indifference

Drifting through life, letting someone else take the initiative, allowing things to happen to you instead of designing a life worth living; these are the hallmarks of indifference; of living by the law of accident rather than by design.

Without active involvement; a goal; a purpose; a sense of direction and the single-minded pursuit of wholistic success, the price we pay for failure can be crushingly expensive. It is not a once-only payment. The terms extend over the rest of your life.

How long do you pay for leading an indifferent lifestyle if you wind up retiring broke? What about the anguish and debt burdens you could suffer in the meantime? Can you rely solely on government handouts when you retire?

Decision Paralysis

It's not the big decisions you take now and then which total success, but the little ones you take every day. Even a book has to be written a page at a time.

Many people fear what might go wrong or worry about criticism so much they will avoid deciding even minor issues.

Even at restaurants they ask others what they are having before deciding on a selection for themselves.

Getting the "I want to think about it" response is one of the great demotivators of salespersons.

Dr Susan Jeffers writes;

"One of the biggest fears that keeps us from moving ahead with our lives is our difficulty in making decisions. As one of my students lamented, "Sometimes I feel like the proverbial donkey between two bales of hay - unable to decide which one I want, and, in the meantime, starving to death." The irony, of course, is that by not choosing, we are choosing - to starve."

(From 'Feel the Fear and Do It Anyway')

The key to understanding decision paralysis is to understand why people are reluctant to make decisions in the first place. In many cases it is simply confusion. People have not understood a proposal or its benefits.

A simple technique for making decisions is to take a plain piece of paper and divide it with a vertical line down the page. On one side of the line list the reasons 'for' the proposal, and on the other side list the reasons 'against'. The better course soon becomes obvious.

Another area of our personal life afflicted by decision paralysis is making up our minds what we want to be. Until we make this decision, progress becomes difficult because we don't know where we are going or if we are going anywhere.

The following steps will help you beat decision paralysis.

- List what you don't want

- List what you might like

- List what you definitely would like, and choose from this list.

Decisiveness is one of the qualities of Self leadership. Don't let fear of making a mistake inflict decision paralysis on you. Consider all the information, separate facts from information, list relevant facts, work out the 'for' and 'against' of the proposal, consider the consequences, then decide.

If you always do what you've always done you'll always get what you've always got.

Worry

Do you know anyone who is troubled by worry? Some people worry about everything. Half the world's heartaches are caused by worry over trifles.

By his timely arrival the Austrian General, Boucher, saved Wellington at Waterloo and helped defeat Napoleon. Yet he worried all his life that he would give birth to an elephant!

Of course we all worry to some extent. If you are in the path of an oncoming train it is wise to worry. This type of worry leads to action.

Someone once said his life had been marred by disasters; most of which never happened.

The great Tolstoy worried so much about hanging himself that he kept a piece of rope hidden from him.

Dr Susan Jeffers says:

"It is reported that 90% of what we worry about never happens. That means that our negative worries have about a 10% chance of being correct. If this is so, isn't it possible that being positive is more realistic than being negative?"

(From 'Feel the Fear and Do It Anyway')

Composer Leonard Bernstein was engaged in a concert tour of the Middle East. He recalls a situation which would have been worrysome for most of us, and what people did about it;

"I gave a downbeat at this morning's rehearsal. It coincided with a perfectly timed explosion outside the hall. We picked ourselves up and calmly resumed our labours.

"We've had four incidents in two days; a kidnapping at this hotel, a train demolished, a police station blown up, a military truck bombed.

"But the cafe-sitters don't put down their newspapers, the children continue to jump rope. The Arab goatherd in the square adjusts another milking bag, and I give the next downbeat."

(From 'Leonard Bernstein' by Joan Peyser)

The moral of that story is not to empower worry (or circumstances) to deflect you from your mission.

Here's a simple formula for handling worry. Write down your answers to the following questions::

What am I worrying about?

- On the laws of probability, what are the chances of this happening to me?

- If it does, what is the worst that can happen?

- Accept the worst as a possibility

Take steps to improve on the worst.

It is often better to accept things you can't change than to worry and stew because they aren't the way you feel they ought to be.

Don't worry about your future: design it instead!

Pessimism

Before the motor car was invented Londoners were told that as traffic increased, within 100 years mountains of horse manure would make the city impassable. Naturally, the pessimists agreed. The curious thing about pessimists is they're seldom right.

It takes the same mental energy to develop the discipline of looking on the bright side of things as it does to look on the dark side. So why bother with pessimism?

Pessimism involves negative self-talk. It affects our views on everything - including ourselves.

Pessimism is a down-payment on a contract to fail.

Many people have burst through the pessimism barrier to achieve inspiring successes; people who could easily be forgiven if they held a very pessimistic view of their future. People like B.P., who became a quadriplegic after a car accident, J.D., who was paralysed by Poliomyelitis, J.B., who was immobilised by severe arthritis, G.B., who became a quadriplegic after a diving accident. All are among members of the Association of Mouth and Foot Paintings Artists; and developed their skills to the point where their work is sold nationally.

Their aim? (published in a leaflet promoting their work) is:

"...to be financially independent - free from charity - and to lead useful, creative, normal lives."

They and others in their group are people who have conquered pessimism and by doing so have achieved success through a high level of Self leadership and Personal Excellence.

Martha Washington said;

"I am still determined to be cheerful and happy in whatever situation I may be, for I have also learned from experience that the greater part of our happiness or misery depends on our dispositions and not on our circumstances."

Pessimistic people tend to be unhappy. (They might be happiest when their dire predictions occur. This justifies their continued self-flagellation.) They have mastered the mentality of the Martyr.

In many instances a pessimistic attitude can ensure its own fulfilment. If you think the world is bright and happy, it is. If you think it is dark and miserable, it is. How can it be otherwise? It's your world. You are creating it.

Stubbornness

Stubbornness is enacting the belief that if you don't give in, the world will mould itself into a shape pleasing to you.

For example, if you are living in an environment marked by fast and frequent change, refusing to adapt won't stop change from occurring.

Be flexible. Don't be afraid of new ideas. Be open to the possibility that others could be right, or at least partly right.

Stubbornness is a barrier. Eventually, barriers are removed.

Stubbornness should not be confused with single-mindedness. Single minded pursuit of your Major Life Goal requires you to be open to any change or idea which can help you attain it.

Stubbornness might be recalling the child who 'held its breath' until he got his own way.

Aesop tells the story of two goats traversing a ravine and meeting on a log . Both insisted they had the right of way and were too stubborn to back off. Eventually they tried to push through and both fell into the ravine.

Henry S. Haskins warns us that;

"A stiff attitude is one of the phenomena of rigor mortis".

Failing to Work Your Plan

How often have you spent hours creating a master plan only to follow it for a little while? Isn't it pointless to work out a plan which you do not intend to follow?

Your plan should be your promise to yourself. The promise for your future. It is you designing the life you want to live; your own storyline. You need to see the promise of your future clearly and want it earnestly or you will not make the effort to achieve it.

Fear of failure or, in some cases, fear of success, can be a major factor in preventing the execution of a plan.

"Plan your work and work your plan", and "If you fail to plan you are planning to fail" may be old cliches but they have stood the test of time.

Low Self-Esteem

Swiss Psychiatrist Alfred Adler coined the term 'Inferiority Complex' to explain our inborn determination to counter feelings of inferiority or low self-esteem. As he put it; our urge to 'turn our minus into a plus'.

We were built for success. How we feel about ourselves is a matter of our own choice.

Eleanor Roosevelt said;

"No one can make you feel inferior without your consent"

Take a few minutes to complete the following suggestion.

Divide a sheet of paper with a vertical line down the centre. Head the left section "Things I like about myself' and the right section "Things I don't like about myself' Complete the lists.

Have you done it?

Good.

Which side has more entries?

If the negative side has more, don't worry. All you have to do is to change one thing and you've already improved.

Master Salesman and Motivator Tom Hopkins talks about self-acceptance as a motivator. He writes;

"Self acceptance is the state of being your own person. You have arrived. Not where somebody else sent you, you have arrived exactly where you want to be. Self-acceptance marks the day when the opinions of other people don't control you anymore. It's the day you start making yourself heard when you don't agree. It's the night you suddenly jump a jet to Europe for a vacation; it's the morning you stay in bed because you want to. It's the hour when you're all through with the games you don't want to play; through with the roles you don't

want to live. It's the minute you finally unlock your potential, become you, know that you've become you, and know that you are completely and gloriously your own person."

(From 'How to Master the Art of Selling')

That could describe much of what it means to be a Self leader. A poor self-esteem does not make for leadership. It even prevents people from becoming good followers.

But if you had such little self-esteem, you would not be studying this course.

By now you will have concluded that we are the architects and master builders of our own barriers. The good news is that as we built them, we can demolish them.

You will know of many cases where attitude made all the difference to the outcome; disabled people who won't give up; sportsmen determined to win; people from all walks of life who strive for and achieve success against incredible odds. They are all strong leaders of self.

All have developed an attitude that life is worth living, that success is worth attaining, that they too are worthy of personal triumph.

Not for them the lethargy, pessimism and quitting attitude of the low achiever. They know that the key to winning in any field is largely a state of mind. This state of mind; or attitude, can be developed until it becomes the way you live every day; *bright, hopeful, energised, happy, successful.*

4

Success Through Personal Growth

Have you ever attended a seminar in which a key speaker outlined how he achieved his extraordinary success? You were full of admiration. Inspired. You might have thought; "Wow! This man has it all; presence, speech, presentation, admiration, achievement". You might also have filled pages with notes, hints; noting each pearl of wisdom as it rolled off his tongue.

Yet when you tried to do the things he does they probably didn't work quite as well for you.

More than likely the speaker was talking from a ten or fifteen year growth perspective while you might have been listening with a two or three year growth experience.

It is almost certain that the way he went about his business at your experience level is markedly different from the way he does his work now.

The difference between you and him was not one of ability, but of personal growth.

In his autobiography; 'Fred Hollows' he tells about the time he failed the same exam twice - six months apart. The reason? In his own words; "I was a boy in a man's game".

He adds that he didn't know enough about ophthalmology, so he decided to do as much practical work as possible to get the experience. He did this extra work for two years, "Working like a dog", then sat for and passed his exams. He said;

"I wasn't trusting to flair and a bit of luck, or blaming the system for anything. I'd grown up, I guess".

In his experience - and achievement - Professor Hollows points the way. It is not enough to know success philosophy or to learn the 'rule book of fundamentals' by heart. We have to do, to learn and apply skills; to grow to the levels of success we want.

There is no greater investment than personal growth.

In Susan Mitchell's book; 'Tall Poppies Too', Carmel Niland describes her 'personal growth';

"One of the things I've always wanted was to like myself. Clearly I never had. I always thought I had to save the world, but now I can like myself for who I am.... At this stage of my life I feel a total connection with my past, present and future, and I have experienced a coming together of things, a wholeness. You could call it a spiritual reaffirmation. What drives me now is joy."

Personal growth begins from the moment we accept that we alone are accountable for our future. Once this is accepted we can take stock of who we are and how we can improve our knowledge, skills and attitudes to achieve success.

It is the moment of self acceptance and commitment to living our own storyline that gives us a first class ticket to our better future.

One of the world's great golfers; Greg Norman, spoke to John Garrity of Time Magazine (Nov 91) about personal growth. He said:

"I'm a country boy, really. I'm not a flamboyant individual. I was a very shy, introverted guy, and I had to change a lot to be successful."

I his life study of success Napoleon Hill found that some of the most successful people had to correct certain weaknesses in their personalities, attitude and beliefs before they began to succeed.

You might need to change not only your thinking and attitudes, but any unproductive habits as well. The process may be stressful - even painful. The result can be stronger Self leadership to wealth, health and happiness.

However all that is easier said than done. I know there are flaws in my personality I would love to change, and I can - temporarily. However in the heat of emotion, of pressure, it's difficult to respond other than through one's conditioning.

This chapter offers some ideas to help you build your own platform for personal growth.

Know Who You Are: Your Personal Totem

It might sound like a cliche but knowing who you are is as essential to success and happiness as sunshine is to flowers.

Try writing down who you are. It will not be as easy as putting down a name and address. For example; what are your core values? What do you believe? How do you see the world around you? What are your attitudes to people? What is your Personal Totem?

Jim MacDonald states;

"In hindsight now, I realise that my first years in sales management with another company were spent in a kind of maze.

"I knew what was required of me - recruiting, training, developing etc, but I didn't have it all together in a useable personal philosophy.

"Changing companies presented me with the opportunity to start afresh and I developed a fairly simple, but for me useful personal philosophy ... whatever its form, it is my belief that a vital ingredient for long term success, is a usable, workable philosophy."

Many tribal people embody 'who they are' by adopting a totem. This can be an eagle, lion, deer, wind, moon, sun etc. Each totem is perceived to have qualities such as strength, speed, courage, wisdom....

By adopting a personal totem the individual adopts its qualities, interprets the daily challenges of life through it and responds to them accordingly.

In our case such qualities can be said to form our core values. These values must not be merely adopted, but believed and defended.

For example, your Totem could represent honesty, integrity, fair play, success only on a win-win basis (Personal Excellence) and so on. The point is that once you have adopted a Totem it will enshrine your code of conduct.

Psychologist Dr Irene C. Kassorla believes honesty is a power tool. She writes:

"You may never have thought of honesty as either a power or a helpful tool, but it is. I believe that honesty is a symbol of strength. It demonstrates high self-esteem and inner feelings of security and dignity. Honesty is magnetic and will draw people to you. They may not be certain why they are attracted to you, but they will like you because honesty is so engaging ..... In my therapy work, I have treated many corporate executives and leaders of Industry. It is interesting to note how many winning characteristics they have in common. Invariably, one of these traits is being honest."

(From: 'Go for It')

Know How You Are: Your Personality

Choosing the right job or business can be a great start to Success. A common factor of successful people is they enjoy what they do.

The wrong choice can lead to considerable financial loss and much unhappiness. For example, an introvert could be unhappy in a position which demanded constant exposure to people; such as in sales.

Why is it that some people are extroverted and others introverted? Why are some people stable and others unstable? Why are some people tender minded and others tough minded?

Psychologists have concluded that a part of our personality is inherited through genes. However upbringing can influence how we turn out. What we can't change is our predominant personality trait.

There are no right or wrong traits. We all have some of each. Your aim should be to discover your predominant trait and to take it into account in your dealings with other people.

(Should you wish to find out 'how' you really are there are many tests provided by professional psychologists.)

Look Out by Looking in

It is a common practice to judge others by our own standards; our own experiences. When we are confronted with a situation or introduced to someone new we immediately invite them to view our travel snap shots; our family album; our 'travelogue'.

In other words we project our own experiences and ideas onto other people and criticise those corners, twists and bumps that don't fit into the picture we have created.

At the same time others have their own travelogue and project it onto us.

Looking back at my own experiences I can see instances where I projected my own standards on others. A simple example was during the time I was an Air Force Officer and long hair for males was all the rage. Given my own background and training, I looked down on men who wore their hair long. I'm ashamed to admit that even years later as a civilian manager, I would turn down a long-haired male for a job in preference to someone who met my 'travelogue' by wearing his hair short.

What a preposterous world view I had. As if the length of hair were some sort of test to identify under-achievers or those who simply didn't fit in. I've grown a lot since those early days, and the biggest lesson of that growth was that I couldn't have grown any faster. Growth takes time.

Individuals are not alone in projecting their own travelogue onto others. Nations do the same thing to other nations! They project their version of history, their set of values, their culture etc., onto their neighbours.

Instead of **valuing** differences we try to beat others into conforming with the travelogue we project upon them.

We expect people to dress as we do, enjoy the same music; sport, food, etc, etc. If they don't, many judge them inferior. Millions of immigrants can explain this point far more eloquently through their experiences.

The most obvious fact about individual differences is that if there were no differences, none of us would be special, or unique, or simply....who we are.

A mark of personal growth is the ability to value differences; to acknowledge that it is the differences that make us special and precious to each other.

By looking inside ourselves before we look at others we might avoid projecting our travelogue and achieve a most blessed release; a release that comes when we stop judging people and start accepting them for who they are.

The Fear of Success

If you are anything like me, initially you will be puzzled that any person would be afraid of success. Yet this fear is one of the major causes of holding back; of being a follower rather than a Self leader.

Zig Ziglar tells the story of a small elephant tied to a post. It cannot break free because the rope is too strong. However when the elephant grows to maturity it could easily break the rope but doesn't try. This is because it has been conditioned to believe it doesn't have the strength.

Our conditioning affects us too. If a person grows within a poor family he might see himself as belonging to that level of society. He might think and act as do the people of his group.

Social pressures to conform will further entrench him with that socio-economic grouping. He might develop a self-identity as a 'worker', 'battler' or as someone who does not 'belong' in any other group.

There's an old saying that no man is a hero to his valet. I learned the truth of this wisdom indirectly as a drummer in a band. The band was popular and we were engaged for many 'upper crust' functions. As the musicians had to drink very moderately for obvious reasons, I was able to observe society's luminaries behaving pretty much like anyone else. I thought that if those were our success stories, captains of industry and political masters, no one need doubt their own ability to fit in.

This was reinforced in my transition from sergeant to commissioned rank. Beforehand I held commissioned officers in awe. When I became one, I felt such a disappointment. They were just like anyone else. My disappointment was so complete that after four years as an officer, I resigned my commission.

The biggest hurdle you have to jump in overcoming the fear of success is to accept that changing any pattern or routine can, initially, be uncomfortable.

Leaving who you are or what you are doing (comfort zone and part of self-identity) to change or do something else, can be risky as well. However fear of risk can also be an echo of conditioning; of living a storyline written by others.

The second biggest hurdle in defeating fear of success is that you have to make a firm resolution to live your own life. I don't mean just in the philosophical sense. I mean it literally. You have to be the master of your fate and accept the responsibility for how your life turns out.

Do you remember the true story of Terry White who changed his job as a sheet-metal worker, became an insurance salesman, succeeded beyond his dreams but tried to take his life?

Had he found the move away from his conditioned 'self' as a sheet-metal worker, too distressing? Too fearful?

We are conditioned to be afraid almost from the time we can walk, and often by well meaning parents and friends (i.e. "Be careful. The world is full of sleazes. You could be mugged/killed, you'll lose all your money/you'll go broke" etc, etc.

Consequently many people sabotage their own success. Not to the extreme that Terry White* tried to do, but through excuses, procrastination, puking, half hearted effort, absenteeism, etc.

Extraordinary as it might seem they do these things to keep themselves within the known; the familiar; within their comfort zone.

Others are too afraid even to try for success. They have been conditioned to think they can't or shouldn't achieve it or are awed by the perception they have of 'successful people' - as was I, until I grew wiser. They have been tied to the post as surely as was the baby elephant in Zig Ziglar's story.

But as you have decided to design you own life and embrace a Totem geared to achieving wealth, health and happiness, you have the *power of purpose.* This power will enable you to lead yourself out of fear-conditioning and into new possibilities for a bright and successful future.

Self-Confidence

Many people who lack self-confidence worry more about what others think of them than what they think of themselves.

The fashion industry makes a fortune by exploiting this fear. How many women would be happy going to an important function in last year's fashions?

Whatever causes a lack of self-confidence; past ridicule, upbringing, fear of criticism, etc., the reality is that few people will pay much attention to you if you don't have confidence in yourself.

Concentrate on what lies ahead. Gather all your experiences and invest them in future successes.

Here are some helpful hints to increase self-confidence.

Planning

Among the worst eroders of self-confidence is lack of planning. If you know you will face a tense situation (eg. giving a talk to a group) *plan* for it.

Know what you are going to do; to say.

Be Prepared

You have already recognised the value of preparation or you would not be studying this course. Researching a topic or problem gives knowledge.

The motto of the Royal Australian Air Force's School of Parachuting is; 'Knowledge Dispels Fear'.

In many cases what unsettles us is fear of the unknown. This generates negative feelings of doubt and worry. The result? Loss of confidence!

Planning and preparation provide this knowledge and give us a feeling of control; of confidence!

Group Activity

By this I mean the time tested confidence-builders such as cross-country hiking, camping, team sports and so on. These can strengthen us physically, socially and spiritually.

Understanding Mistakes

A missile 'learns' by registering successes. The only way it can do this is by experiencing mistakes (i.e. veering off-course).

The corrections (decisions) it makes to stay on-course are its responses to those 'mistakes' and lead it to its goal.

Greg Norman says of mistakes;

"Whether I've played exceptionally well or poorly, I've always been able to proceed as if nothing had happened. What's the point of crying over spilt milk? It's just going to create more anguish between your ears."

(Interview by John Garrity; 'Time', Nov 91)

Mistakes are never a sign for us to quit, but a time to gather what we have learned from experience and invest it in our future.

Buck Duke, founder of Duke University and a chain of retail stores, said of mistakes;

"A mistake? I've made mistakes all my life. And if there is one thing that's helped me, it's the fact that when I make a mistake I never stop to talk about it. I just go ahead and make some more!"

The person who never makes mistakes usually doesn't make anything.

The Power Within You

Jack Canfield, President of Self-Esteem Seminars, developed an amazing demonstration of the power of a positive mental attitude. Dr Susan Jeffers relates it in her book; 'Feel the Fear and Do It Anyway'. She writes:

"I ask someone to come up and stand facing the rest of the class. After making sure the person has no problems with his or her arms. I ask my volunteer to make a fist and extend either arm out to the side."

"I then tell her to resist, with as much strength as she can muster as I stand facing her (attempting) to push her arm down with my outstretched hand. Not once have I succeeded in pushing (her) arm down on my initial trial."

Dr Jeffers then asks the volunteer to put her arm down, close her eyes and repeat ten times "I am a weak and unworthy person". She repeats the arm experiment and is able to bring the volunteer's arm down immediately.

Dr Jeffers asks the volunteer to close her eyes again and repeat ten times "I am a strong and worthy person". To everyone's amazement, she cannot even budge the volunteer's arm!

I have carried out the same experiment many times, and it has always worked.

It demonstrates the awesome power we hold within our mind to influence our abilities and actions.

Just as we have the power to choose, we also have the ability to *empower.*

It means that we can give power to those things which are positive and helpful to our Major Life Goal, and refuse to empower those things which are negative and harmful.

Whilst it is difficult to choose a calm response; to ignore and therefore not empower a situation when emotions are involved, it can be done. You can't change how you feel but you can change what you do about it.

The power is not in mere words or events, but within ourselves; in how we choose to respond and in so doing whether or not to give power to harm us.

Read the Books

I love good books. In fact, one of my most treasured possessions is a personal library of some 1000 books collected over 25 years. I decided very early in my working life that the best education I could get would be the education I could give myself - and this wouldn't include memorising the annual rainfall in Peru, drawing maps of the British Isles or the study of any subject which did not interest me.

I was interested in people and what made so many of them extraordinary.

Through this self-education programme I learned that success leaves clues everywhere, so I decided to learn from the experiences of successful people.

Others who came to the same decision include; Henry Ford, Thomas Edison who said; "I devoted every cent, regardless of future needs, to scientific books and materials for experiments", Simon Lake (developer of the Submarine) Dwight Eisenhower (Supreme Commander of Allied Forces in WWII and later President of the U.S.A.) Robert E. Peary (discover of the North Pole) novelist Rudyard Kipling and many, many more winners were inspired towards their goal by a single book.

Others such as novelist Edgar Wallace read the dictionary from cover to cover; so did Millard Fillmore (President of the U.S.A.), playwright Laurence Bassett, British Prime Minister William Pitt, writer O. Henry and many other noted achievers. Their command of words made them outstanding communicators.

Even King Solomon himself advised: *"Buy learning, and wisdom, and understanding"*

Self leaders must have read King Solomon's advice too, because almost invariably, they are readers.

Humour Yourself

Most people identify humour with the telling of jokes. However that is not what I mean by 'humouring oneself'. In my definition, maintaining a sense of humour means taking our work seriously, but ourselves lightly.

The ability to take ourselves lightly can preserve our reason in the most tense situations. For example, when legendary comedian Jack Benny was held up by a gunman and asked for his 'money or his life'. Jack didn't reply straight away. When pressed, he answered:

"I'm thinking it over! I'm thinking it over".

On being deposed from his throne King Farouk of Egypt said;

"There will soon be only five kings left; the king of England, Diamonds, Hearts, Spades and Clubs".

Playwright Oscar Wilde, handcuffed and standing in pouring rain on the way to prison, took himself lightly when he told his guard;

"If this is the way Queen Victoria treats her prisoners, she doesn't deserve to have any!"

The ability to look at life in perspective, not over-reacting at every trifle, seeing humour in the things we and others do - including our folly; that is what I mean by humouring ourselves. It can save our life.

Humouring oneself is covered a little more in depth later in the course. In the meantime the following verse by American poet Ella Wheeler Wilcox makes a point well worth remembering:

'Tis easy enough to be pleasant
When life flows by like a song
But the man worthwhile
Is the man with a smile
When everything goes dead wrong"

Your List of Required Success Skills

In addition to what has already been covered, most successful people have skills in:

- Human relations

- Negotiation

- Influencing others and winning co-operation

- Public speaking

- Managing money and making it grow

- Time management

- Business plans/personal goal plans

- Developing a win-win instinct

- Handling 'moments of truth'

- Self-motivation

If it all sounds like too much effort; too much Self leadership, there is an old Bohemian proverb which might help to focus our thoughts;

"The time will come when winter will soon ask us;
What were you doing all summer?"

For me, winter will be old age; that time when we've used up our second chances; when we mostly live in our memories. That winter will ask; *"What did you do with your life?"* I don't want to reply: *"If only...."* or *"I could have been..."* I want to be able to look life in the mirror and say: *"I scripted the life I wanted, then lived it."*

How about you?

Book Two

Applied Success Knowledge And Skills

5

Success in Human Relations

An American study asked 100 males selected at random to rate themselves on their ability to get along with other people. All of them rated themselves in the top 50%. 60% of them rated their abilities in the top 10% and one in four placed themselves in the top 1%. (From 'In Search of Excellence' by Thomas J Peters and Robert H Waterman.)

The point is that most of us like to think ourselves successful in our relationships with others. But is it true? And if we are not so successful, does it really matter?

I believe it matters a great deal because human issues aside, *we succeed best when we are able to get other people's best.* That happens when people *want* to do the things we ask of them, not when they *have* to do them.

Most successful people regard their ability to get along with others as one of their chief assets. Some say it *is* their chief asset. They put a major effort into enhancing human relations in their business.

For them, good human relations is a philosophy, not a tactic.

In the words of Immanuel Kant;

"Every man is to be respected as an absolute end in himself, and it is a crime against the dignity that belongs to him as a human being to use him as a mere means for some external purpose".

If we are to achieve wholistic success we need to appreciate the value of other people; their contribution to our mutual success and their right to grow with us.

Yet a great many people who in a moment of reflection might agree with these principles, abandon them utterly when dealing with their employees, customers or with the community at large. Why not prove it for yourself? It would be a safe bet that if you were to ask 100 people whether they believed in 'respect for the individual', at least 99 of them would say "Yes".

So why do so many people say one thing and do another?

Many training programmes teach people to be financial controllers, accountants, engineers...... but how many teach human relations? Are people only 'consumers of food and producers of excrement?'

My own research indicates that how well you get on with other people depends largely on how you perceive them in relation to how you see yourself. That's where it all seems to start.

America's pilgrim fathers perceived the American Indians as savages who failed to make proper use of their land. Thus they justified taking it from them.

When the British claimed Australia they conveniently ignored the Aborigines who had lived there for the preceding 60,000 years, by declaring the continent, 'Uninhabited'. They perceived the Aborigines as 'non existent'; or as fauna.

How could those people - most of whom were churchgoers who perceived themselves as good Christian folk - have failed so miserably in human relations on such a large scale?

The answer could lie in a game we all tend to play:

Labelling

Generals talk of people who are soldiers as 'military assets' 'casualties', 'personnel', 'infantry' etc. Labelling others masks their humanity and enables our conscience to cope with the injustices we inflict on each other.

Why don't newscasters report the 'People toll'? Instead, they use the term 'Road Toll'. But it is people who are injured or die.

Ellis Island was the gateway to 'The tired, the poor, the huddled masses yearning to breathe free' who emigrated to America. How did some Americans perceive the new arrivals? They met them as they came ashore and exchanged their European money - their life savings - for counterfeit American dollars!

The victims weren't people; they were immigrants! That perception helped make the difference.

The device of labelling is also used to help make actions more acceptable. For example, the Bosnian Serbs justified bombing their Muslim minority in Bosnia Hercegovena out of their homes through a label they called 'Ethnic Cleansing'.

Perceptions guide - and help mask - actions. To succeed in human relations we need to have a human perception of ourselves then learn to see our own humanity in others; to see past the labels.

Succeeding in human relations might not be entirely essential to making money, but it is essential to happiness; to living a satisfying and fulfilling life.

We are gregarious creatures. Few of us can be content in a life of social or physical solitude. To be truly happy we need companionship. We tend to enjoy beautiful things when we have someone to whom we can say; "Isn't that something?" Sharing ourselves, our feelings and achievements seems to be a fundamental need of the human psyche. So if we need each other, doesn't it make sense to learn how to get along together?

To do this we need a good understanding of how we - and other people - think and behave.

How Do You See Other People?

As General Manager of a large holiday resort complex one of my tasks was to hold monthly meetings which involved about 100 staff. In the weeks before each meeting I would analyse progress to date and any issues to be resolved. Before the meeting I would have all the answers and plans to implement them.

I couldn't understand why many of the staff didn't appreciate my efforts. After all, I always considered their welfare. Had I not done them a favour by saving them the effort of having to work things out for themselves? Hadn't I put in 12 to 14 hour days preparing all the material for them? Why weren't they more appreciative?

One day I read Dale Carnegie's book; 'How to Win Friends and Influence People'. What a revelation! It wasn't that I had ungrateful staff; the problem was me.

Unwittingly, I perceived my staff as incapable; unable to solve problems; unable to contribute. Worse, in between the lines I must have signalled inadvertantly that I didn't appreciate or value them. The way I perceived them triggered my response which to their ears must have sounded like;

"I have absolutely no confidence in you. You couldn't possibly solve even the most minor problems so I have done it all for you. This is how you will do it .... etc."

What an oaf! My good intentions did not mitigate my actions at all! If I had grown enough to realise this (or had I read Dale Carnegie's book sooner!) I would not have caused myself so much anguish. I would have benefited from the talents of my staff and the place would have been a happier environment producing even better results.

To this day I feel ashamed when I think how blind I was, and how patronising my management style had been.

Consider the view of the television advertiser. How does he see people? Does he see them as humans or as consumers? How do advertisements talk to you? Do you deserve to be congratulated because you buy a specific brand of margarine? Are you clever because you use a specific laundry detergent? Do you win sex with beautiful people if you drink *'Superfizz'*?

How do others see people?

Salespersons might see them as *prospects.*

The police might see them as *suspects.*

Shopkeepers might see them as *customers.*

Airline workers might see them as *passengers.*

Industrialists might see them as *labour.*

Politicians might see them as *voters.*

Does that sound too far fetched? Let's see.

1991 was a year of severe drought in Queensland Australia. The Capital; Brisbane, recorded its longest period without rain. However this four month bounty of clear skies did not please all residents.

When I took my car to a panelbeater I asked him how things were going.

"Terrible" he sighed. "No rain - fewer accidents - bad for business. I hope we get rain real soon!".

To that particular panelbeater people were customers. Never mind about injury, shattered families and trauma.

Of course, not all panelbeaters take such a selfish view. All I am saying is that it is too easy to see others through the looking glass of our own travelogue and to label them accordingly.

Shouldn't we see each other for what we all are; people? Should we not seek to ascertain the content of a person's character rather than project our own travelogue onto them then gripe about the parts that don't fit? Should we not seek to understand rather than to judge? Should we not lead ourselves to this facet of Personal Excellence?

How Do People See Themselves?

Most people are annoyed when others dump litter onto the roadside, start their lawn mower at seven a.m. on Sunday, damage property and so on. They ask; *"How can they do these things? Don't they have a conscience?"*

Well, yes and no.

Nearly everyone regards themselves as basically good. If you were to criticise most people for their actions they would either suggest where you should go or rationalise: they had to start the mower at 7 a.m. because they would be going out for the day; they had to dump that litter on the side of the road because they didn't know the location of the nearest bin; they had to rob that bank, sell that drug, beat that person etc.

The more you criticise them, the more they defend their position. Consequently it's almost useless criticising anyone for anything. Criticism is unlikely to change their behaviour and can breed resentment for a lifetime.

Seldom do we blame ourselves for anything and we certainly detest uninvited criticism from others. The fact is that most of us feel superior to others in some way.

If we lead ourselves to listen with the intent to understand rather than with the intent to reply, we might discover the other person's viewpoint. At that moment progress becomes possible. At that moment Personal Excellence is reinforced.

How Well Do You Like People?

Generally if you are really interested in people they will like you. They will also be more co-operative and willing to 'buy' what you have to 'sell'.

The question is; how can you like others if you simply ... don't?

It's dangerous to fake interest in others to win their favour. This transforms genuine human interest into a device for our own ends. Inevitably, when placed under pressure our true nature breaks out for all to see.

To like others you will need to like yourself. To like yourself you will need to base your life on core values of integrity, fair dealing and honesty.

One of my favourite sayings is: "God invented people because he liked to listen to stories". The seed of developing a sincere liking for your fellow humans lies within that saying.

Talk to people. Listen empathically. Ask questions about things which interest them. You will soon realise that even the 'dull and ignorant' have their story and more often than not, it is a very good one.

Give Others a Good Feeling About Themselves

One of the marvellous things about dogs is they live for affection. Regardless of what sort of day you've had at work your dog will always be glad to see you; eager to give and receive love.

The other great thing about dogs is they give love without a 'catch'. They are not trying to sell you anything or flatter you to get their own way.

It's little wonder that dogs have earned the reputation as man's best friend.

We can learn a lot about getting on with people from man's best friend; namely, be glad to see people. Treat people you meet as if they were guests in your home. Make them feel important.

Isn't that the way you would like to be treated?

Most of us are just like you!

The Vital Art of Person to Person Communication

When you go to a social gathering, what type of person do you find boring or irritating? Isn't he the one who spends all evening talking about himself? What he did, what he wants, what he thinks? They don't give us a chance to talk about what we did, what we want, what we think.

If only conversations were just like the speech in books; one talks, the other listens, then replies. It's all very orderly. Everyone has a turn. But in reality things are seldom like that.

Often two or three people have *parallel* conversations; talking about different things at the same time.

For example, Mother A talks about Johnny's excellent efforts at football on the week end, while Mother B listens, then replies with a statement about her Billy's tennis match. Mother A retorts with another salvo about Johnny while Mother B replies with a rejoinder about Billy. It's all smooth, conversational, friendly and all smiles. Yet the two women are talking with - not to - each other.

Because empathic listening is so rare we enjoy a sense of importance when others really want to listen to what we have to say.

Yet many people listen with the intent to reply or for words that enable them to steer the conversation in the direction they want. It is little wonder that for those people, smooth and relaxed conversations elude them.

Is there a trick to achieving effective person to person communication? To relaxing people at the outset? To getting them to talk? To being a good conversationalist?

The answer is yes, but as for anything else, the art of making good conversation takes effort and practice to master.

Note the following discourse overheard at a party:

He: *Did you watch the football yesterday?*

She: *No*

He: *Aren't you interested in football?*

She: *Not really.*

He:(Changing subject) *Have you known (the hosts) long?*

She: *No*

He: *I've known them for years. In fact, I first met them* .... (and off he went talking about himself)

There are several problems with the structure of this type of conversation. He was on the right track by asking questions.

However they were 'closed' questions; the kind that can be answered with a 'Yes' or 'No'. So the conversation was awkward, stilted and uncomfortable.

He then changed the subject onto himself hoping the conversation might go more smoothly. The overall problem was that he talked in terms of his interests rather than hers.

Asking questions and *listening empathically* are the two most vital keys to effective person to person communication. However to generate conversation that is relaxed, smooth and flowing we need to ask *open* questions; questions which encourage a fluent response; questions which start with; **what, where, how, when, why** or **who.**

The previous conversation might have progressed in the following way if 'he' had used any one of those open 'question starters'.

He: *What did you think of the football yesterday?*

She: *I didn't watch it, really.*

He: *Oh? That's a pity. It was a great game. How often do you get to see the home matches?*

She: *I don't. I'm afraid football doesn't really interest me.*

He: *Oh? What sports do interest you?*

This is not a 'great' conversation by any means but it flows easily and both people feel relaxed. At least he is trying to find out her interests.

Why not try it? Use any of the six 'open' dialogue starters. Be sincere in your interest. People will see you as charming and as good company provided you listen empathically to their answers.

At work there might be an additional factor which can block good person to person communication; low morale. In those circumstances hardly any communication can take place because one party (staff) doesn't really want to listen. They don't even want to be there!

In those cases morale needs to improve before effective communication can take place.

Arguments

The best way to win an argument is to avoid it. Even if you prove your point correct, when you win an argument; you lose. That is because when you win you've struck a body blow at the other person's ego; a blow which will not be forgiven.

You can't change people's opinions. They need to change them for themselves. Time shows again and again that the way to help others see your point of view is to show a sympathetic grasp of their point of view.

Saying to someone, "You're wrong!" is not likely to influence their opinion one bit; quite the reverse. They will become defensive and resent you.

In many cases it is our own attitude which leads to arguments. Instead of valuing differences we pounce on them and try to stifle them. Fear of differences can lead to extremes such as the Inquisition and the Holocaust.

Is it that difficult to say in a warm and sincere manner something like; *"You have a different view? Great! Help me to understand how you see it"*.

An effective start to dealing with a difference of opinion is by beginning in a friendly tone. For example;

"I see your point. In many cases I think that would be quite right. But on this occasion it seems to me that......" or "I could be wrong. Let's look at the facts together ......"

That is much better than;

"I disagree! How can you have the gall to say that when you know .....etc." or

"You're way off beam! Couldn't be more wrong!" etc.

Often we might argue over a statement which, in itself, may not be the true bone of contention. What we might be objecting to may be the tone in which it was said, or the manner in which it was conveyed. Many arguments can be avoided by good manners and gentle words.

Start friendly. Listen empathically with the intent to understand and not with the intent to reply. If you are wrong, admit it with good grace. You will be respected for it.

Arrogance and Rudeness

Again, how we respond to people comes down to the way we perceive them in relation to ourselves. You might have seen examples of people who are charming and polite to a boss, but quite rude to the secretaries or office clerks. The perception there is that secretaries and clerks aren't important.

Not only is rudeness counter-productive, it is utterly unnecessary and reflects sadly on the person giving it.

Arrogance, on the other hand, comes from a feeling of superiority over others.

Philosophers can fall for that trap too, as the great Immanuel Kant pointed out;

"I am myself by inclination a seeker after truth. I feel a consuming thirst for knowledge and a restless passion to advance in it...... There was a time when I thought this alone could constitute the honour of mankind, and I despised the common man who knows nothing.

"Rousseau set me right...... I learned to respect human nature, and I should consider myself far more useless than the ordinary workingman if I did not believe that this view (respect for the individual) could give worth to all others to establish the rights of man".

(From '100 Great Thinkers', Simon & Schuster, Heron Books)

The story of the visit to Papua New Guinea by the Leahy brothers includes an encounter with 'hidden' tribes. The natives were amazed at how the brothers survived. After all they neither hunted nor fished. Over time the natives began to see the Leahy brothers as 'gods' or as 'spirits of their dead ancestors'.

One day their perception changed. The Chief, with his most respected warriors secretly followed the Leahy brothers and observed them defecating. Afterwards the Chief and his entourage went to inspect the excrement. At once the Chief observed; *"It smells just like ours!"*

I hope you will forgive this crude, but true example. It does make the point that arrogance has no place in human relations.

The Human Relations Trust Account

Stephen R Covey's view expressed in his book 'The Seven Habits of Highly Effective People' is that we build 'Trust' accounts.

In other words, my friendship and prior interaction with you has won trust and confidence. Everytime I do something which builds on this, I deposit more trust into my account with you.

Whenever I do something which asks you to accept it on trust, you make a withdrawal from my account.

Your account might have healthy trust deposits with family and friends, but what about with your fellow workers? How does your human relations balance look with employees, associates and other people in business?

Consider the situation where a person is falsely accused of a misdemeanour at work. If the balance in his human relations trust account is high, would not the company stand firmly by him?

What if the account were bankrupt?

Employee Human Relations

How we treat employees is determined by our perception of them. For example if our emphasis is on the financial sphere of life we could regard them as 'labour' to do our bidding - another label masking their humanity!

People 'volunteer' to work with us. We do not own them. If we treat them as volunteers, they will volunteer their best efforts in our behalf.

Whether at work or at home, the value we place on human relations is a reflection of our own self-value.

People are all we've got, so why not give them honest and sincere appreciation? We're sure to get some right back.

Postscript

There is, to be honest, one unspoken rule; you can't win them all. The ideas offered in this chapter will work *most* of the time. Much depends on the level of our personal growth.

I once had a neighbour who was a builder. Building work was short, and I needed an expensive extension for my house. Because he was a next door neighbour I didn't bother getting quotes. I gave him the job and all progress payments with alacrity.

When the work was done he had overcharged me by $1200 for bricks which were neither delivered nor laid. Naturally, I assumed this to be a simple error and using my best human relations approach talked it over with him, being sure to leave him a face-saving 'out'.

But he refused to look at the work.

I tried again, calmly and in a friendly manner, saying that I would be happy to pay him the extra if he insisted, provided he would first see if an honest error had been made. Many groans. Total intransigence.

To my discredit I threw away everything I knew of good human relations, influencing people and so on, and told him that if he didn't come over to see for himself, I could only assume that he *deliberately cheated me* - his own next-door neighbour.

He retorted that I was trying to cheat him, and we both lost our cool. I paid him the total amount, less a compromise of $800, with a note telling him that as soon as he could show me the extra bricks, I would pay him the balance AND take him and his wife out to dinner.

The result? A neighbour with whom we don't talk.

The fault? Mine. I could have handled it better. I could have 'walked my talk'. I could have appealed to his sense of honour. The problem was that I hadn't yet reached a sufficient level of personal growth.

Whenever we are placed under pressure, our true feelings can emerge. That's why it so important to make an effort until we respond with Personal Excellence as a reflex action.

And even then I suspect we won't win them all. Why? Because the other party's level of personal growth also influences the outcome. The important thing is that we do our best. We'll win far more than we lose and reinforce our Personal Excellence in the process.

6

Influencing Others - Winning Co-Operation

Sir Edmund Hillary and the Sherpa, Tensing, were the first people to climb Mount Everest. But to achieve their historic feat of endurance, courage and perseverance they needed the co-operation of 40 Sherpa guides and 700 porters.

To achieve almost anything, including wealth, we need the ability to work with others; to influence them and to win their co-operation.

Working with others is not like driving a bus where you are behind the steering wheel and everyone gets to where you steer. It's more like being in a vehicle which has lots of steering wheels - but only one belongs to you. The object is to get everyone to want to steer in the same direction.

So how do you influence people to want to do something you want done and have them like it?

Cigarette companies are experts at influencing people. They raised smoking to celebrity status. Indeed, cigarettes have been called the world's cheapest status symbol. By linking cigarettes to 'beautiful people', outdoors, film stars, sports events etc they influence countless people - including the young - to equate smoking with status and lifestyle.

Pierre Cardin made his fortune by creating designer clothes for the affluent and famous then promoting his label around the world. The result? He sold 'celebrityhood'. When people buy the PC label they buy status. They want others to be impressed with their purchase.

We all have the ability to influence other people. Those who develop this ability usually are promoted more swiftly, succeed more quickly and to a greater extent.

How do some people evoke deep feelings of loyalty in their employees? How do they influence them to perform unpleasant tasks and work long hours willingly?

Australian Airlines is a carrier which had captured a relatively minor share of the business market. Through an imaginative advertising campaign based on the friendliness and co-operation of their staff they reversed their plight to become the market leader in Australia within a very short time.

Over 150 staff volunteered to take part in taping a television commercial. With takes and re-takes they remained on the cold tarmac until 3am, with no pay, no complaint and only an airline meal as recompense.

Wives and husbands had also been waiting to take their spouses home, but all remained to help the company build its image.

What is the philosophy that can build such loyalty?

Many successful men and women will tell you that one of their most important assets is their ability to influence others.

I am not talking of 'manipulation' or cajolery. I am talking about a more satisfying human interaction; about a philosophy, not a tactic. This means leading others to co-operate by creating win-win situations.

A 'win' for the other person is one that reinforces his sense of self-esteem, recognises his humanity, enhances his feeling of being appreciated or benefits him materially.

The win-win philosophy is far more effective than using fear or threats.

Whilst it is true in most cases that if you threaten to dismiss an employee the task will get done, it will be done in a grudging, resentful way.

The result? Staff who aim to do only the minimum, who usually need further threats to motivate them and who will have little or no loyalty to you or to your business.

This style of 'influencing' creates a dispirited and unhappy atmosphere. Often the solution employed by senior management is to dismiss the manager.

In an age where people tend to be loyal to their profession rather than to their company, developing the skill to win co-operation is even more important.

To earn co-operation we need to co-operate. We might have to meet others half-way; give in to a minor point to win a major one; compromise.

Why?

Because there is only one way to get others to do something well, swiftly and cheerfully; they must want to do it. There is no other way.

How is it done? Here are some suggestions:

The Sweetest Sound

The most important thing to us, is us! Our ears prick up whenever we hear our name. It has a sweet sound which we value above music. It is ours. It is us. Morning, noon and night, we love the sound of our name.

When our name is called we listen attentively to the sentence which follows it. Teachers use it to get our attention. Good conversationalists use our name often. We lap it up.

Roger Viard, director of the famous French restaurant, Maxims, addressed clients by name, knew their special demands and where they liked to be seated. So if you want to influence people and win their co-operation one of the very basic requirements is to use their name.

This is not always easy. Our natural inclination to size each other up when first introduced means that most of us forget the person's name immediately. So we cop out by pleading "I'm terrible with names."

The truth is there is no such thing as a bad memory; only a lack of Self-leadership. For salespeople, remembering and using names is a vital element of sales success. Here's the 'I.R.A.' formula for improving your name-memory.

Impression

When you first meet someone, get a clear impression of his face and name. Link the two together in your mind. If it's appropriate, ask them to repeat it or to spell it.

Repetition

Repeat his name to yourself (and use it) at short intervals.

Association

Associate his name and face with a mental picture, preferably a moving picture. (The more ridiculous the association, the easier it is to remember it.)

So the first rule of influencing people and winning co-operation is to make a practice of remembering and using names. Jot them down. Ask people to spell them so you can form a stronger impression. Use names often so they will be imprinted in your mind. (Use your imagination to link their name with their most prominent feature.)

If we can't remember the other person's name how can we expect them to remember us?

Smile

Have you heard of the man who fell in love with a smile and wound up marrying the whole person? It may be a humorous extreme, but it illustrates the powerful influence of a smile.

Smiles are free! They make it almost impossible to be angry while smiling in a heartfelt way.

Research shows that people who smile often tend to lead fuller, happier lives, raise happier children and for salespeople; sell more.

When we smile we signal to others that we are friendly and glad to see them.

So when you meet someone who's run out of smiles, give them one of yours. (They'll give it straight back!)

Appeal to Peoples' Sense of Honour

We often do things to live up to other people's faith in us.

Sometimes appealing to one's honour can influence the most unco-operative individual. Consider the following conversation:

Boss: *"John, the company's going through a rough patch. But we can pull out of it by working together."*

Supervisor: *"What do you mean?"*

Boss: *"You're in charge of a good team. But the results they're bringing in are lower than those of other teams - and they've got fewer men. We need increased productivity from everybody."*

Supervisor: *"I don't know who you've been talking to, but I can tell you we're all working our tails off."*

Boss: *"I'm not saying you're not working hard. What we've got to do is work smart."*

Supervisor: *"What are you getting at?"*

Boss: *"John, I know you'll do whatever it takes to help. If you have to get new staff, I'll back your judgement. Meanwhile take a look at how you can improve your team's work practices. Talk to other team leaders. Find out what they're doing. I know I can rely on you."*

I am sure you can think of many examples where this principle could apply. There's nothing wrong with trying to influence an outcome by appealing to a person's honour. It has the added benefit of building their self-image and reinforcing positive values.

Appealing to honour, coupled with a demonstration of faith in the person, is far more effective than using fear tactics. It creates an environment of co-operation and goodwill.

At the conclusion of the American Civil War, victorious general Ulysses S. Grant told President Abraham Lincoln: *"I was successful because you had faith in me."*

We All Love Ideas

Have you ever presented what you knew was a great idea but failed to win support for it?

To win others to our way of thinking we need to appeal to their imagination. We need to impress our idea so it will not be forgotten or buried with all the others vying for attention.

For example, imagine you were selling a new seat belt on the basis of its great strength. Would it be effective to table a list of specifications including stress tests, material, comparisons etc? This might gain you some sales, but how long would it take for your competitor to win business away from you, or for your product to be forgotten?

Appeal to imagination! Why not have a helicopter lift a car by a single seat belt? You won't need statistics to convince anyone of your product's strength. More importantly, they would remember the image you created for a very long time. The publicity would be an added plus.

Author Colleen McCullough discovered that even back in 1972 Random House received 7000 unsolicited manuscripts each week. When she wanted to publish her first novel 'Tim' she decided to go through a literary agent. However agents are not usually interested in unpublished authors.

Rather than send yet another unsolicited manuscript, Colleen McCullough decided to write her selected agent the best letter an agent had ever seen, on the theory she would consent to read the manuscript *"Only if my letter showed her what a terrific writer I was."*

The subject of her letter was *"How I hated cleaning the stove."* It worked!

Appealing to imagination is stock in trade for advertisers, film directors and entertainers.

So when next you are presenting an idea, use flair! Don't *say* your idea will sell twenty more cakes for every two sold now; take 22 cakes to your sales presentation. Place two on one side of the table and 20 on the other.

Get the idea? They will!

Nothing Succeeds Like Reward

W.I.I.F.M? (What's in it for me?) is alive and well in all of us.

Reward need not be monetary. It could be recognition, appreciation, esteem or satisfaction.

We do things because we get something out of it. We give money to charity for a feeling of unselfishness. (Sometimes we do it to prevent a feeling of embarrassment when asked for money in front of others.)

Whatever we do, we do it because of W.I.I.F.M.

If we know that people crave appreciation and reward, doesn't it make sense to provide it?

Thomas J Watson, founder of I.B.M., believed that the way to win people's loyalty was by bolstering their self-respect. His son, Thomas J Watson Jr., later to become chairman of IBM, learned the importance of bolstering self respect when he saw how his lack of self confidence was transformed by his Air Force boss; General Bradley.

In his book, 'Father, Son and Co', he writes;

"On (my) reports General Bradley would often scrawl; 'Thank you very much', and sometimes 'Excellent' or even 'Splendid'

- small compliments that drove me to do an even better and more vigorous job. My months with Bradley were among the most important of my life because he showed me I had an orderly mind and an unusual ability to focus on what was important and put it across to others."

When other people reward us with faith and confidence we tend to rise to meet their expectations.

For many years Christian Dior was the world's guru of fashion. He made a special point of giving credit to others such as his head tailor, a young man named Pierre Cardin. He said to Pierre publicly; *"Take up the torch. It can be yours."*

Another of Christian Dior's talented staff was a young man named Yves Saint Laurent. Christian Dior made sure the fashion world recognised the talent of his gifted employees. Passing credit to others is a great reward for the giver and the receiver.

Rewarding each success - no matter how small - is an effective way to reinforce the kind of co-operation we want. It also provides a good feeling and sense of achievement for the person rewarded. It builds success patterns.

Next time you want to influence someone to co-operate, ask yourself; W.I.I.F.H? (What's in it for him?) Credit? Appreciation? Recognition? Importance? Material gain? If there are none of those, chances are they will not be influenced to co-operate at all.

Some People Can't Resist a Challenge

Sometimes we try our best to influence others but to no avail. Why not give them a challenge? Why not appeal to their ego?

The rewards in meeting a challenge are recognition and achievement. (It often helps to have a material reward as well.) Competitions are largely based on this principle just as 'bonuses' are given for achieving work quotas.

A boss might allocate a junior officer to a more senior position. The challenge is for that officer to handle the job successfully.

In the meantime the boss makes it clear that if the junior succeeds, a promotion could result.

The individual who says he can't be bothered with a challenge is probably afraid of failure and is making excuses ahead of time. Another version of 'Wooden Leg!'

Do You Want a Good Reputation?

It might be true that some people enjoy reputations they do not deserve - good or bad. How often do we hear that a public figure has been charged with a criminal offence? How often are people maligned by gossip and rumour?

Given the option we would all choose a fine reputation. We all want to enjoy respect and admiration.

You might have seen the principle of appealing to a person's reputation at work. A president or secretary in charge of a meeting will thank 'Mr Jones' for his outstanding contribution to a particular effort and might add: *"He always produces outstanding results."*

It follows that more often than not, Mr Jones will try to live up to his reputation.

If you have an important task to be done but feel you won't be overwhelmed with volunteers, you could try the following approach;

"(John,) I need someone who can be relied on to get things done. I know you're very busy, but I couldn't trust this job to someone less reliable" ..... etc.

Giving people a good reputation to live up to builds their self esteem and lets them know their skills are recognised and appreciated.

Everybody wins when you take that approach.

The Art of Counselling

Counselling others, drawing attention to their mistakes indirectly and admonishing in a supportive, constructive way while letting them retain their dignity; that is a hallmark of Personal Excellence.

When we are counselled we expose our ego to attack. We become emotionally vulnerable. In those sensitive circumstances everyone feels uncomfortable.

Here are some suggestions to lessen discomfort, preserve dignity and win co-operation:

- Find something you can praise about the person. Express your appreciation for his efforts. Be specific. Mention instances.

- Talk about some of *your* past mistakes.

- Discuss the problem area. Listen empathically to his point of view. Make the problem appear easy to fix. Preferably, ask for his suggestions. If necessary, help him find ways to fix it.

- Praise his good points again and encourage him to keep up his good work. Let him know you're pleased he's in your team and that you have confidence in his ability to fix the problem.

If you want to modify a person's behaviour you'll succeed only if he wants to modify it. The challenge is to lead him to want to do so.

No One Likes To Be Ordered

We all prefer being asked to being ordered.

It is often helpful to remember that leaders get to the top largely on the efforts of those below them!

If people choose to invest a third or more of their life in working for you it does not mean you own them. We 'buy' their labour, we don't 'buy' them.

We gain much more by winning their loyalty; by making them want to co-operate; by treating them as volunteers.

If you do not like orders it should come as no surprise that other people don't like them either.

Instead of barking: "Do this!" or "Do that!", try something like; "Could you please . . ." and add "Thanks".

Truly successful people don't give orders. They suggest. For example:

"Could you give some thought as to how we might ..." and again "Do you think... could be more effective?"

That approach avoids resentment and grudging acceptance. It treats people with dignity and creates a happier work environment.

General Ike Eisenhower, Commander in Chief of the Allies during World War Two and later President of the United States, had all the authority anyone could ask. Did he go around ordering people? According to Stephen E Ambrose; "Eisenhower's method was to lead through persuasion and hints, rather than through direct action."

The man who *could* order, preferred to ask, hint, suggest.

Aesop wrote a fable which I believe encapsulates the essence of effective human interaction. Here's a paraphrase:

The wind saw a man in an overcoat walking along a dusty road and said to the sun:

"I bet I can force that man to take off his coat!"

So he blew and blew and created a mighty wind. But the stronger the wind, the more tightly the man held onto his coat.

Finally it was the sun's turn. With a smile he increased the warmth of the air. Feeling the kindly warmth the man willingly removed his coat.

Kindliness is more effective than bluster.

Meetings

Do you call a meeting to find out *what* others think, or to tell them *what to* think?

Consider the following:

Boss: *"Thanks for coming to today's meeting. As you know, our target for this quarter is less than half way to being met and we only have three weeks to do something about it! So what you will do is this, that and the other . .".*

Is that reminiscent of meetings you have attended? I'm ashamed to say those are like the meetings I used to run!

That approach leads to some of the key failures of meetings. That is:

a)   *'Group Think'* where no one will air doubts or say anything which could threaten the harmony of the group.

b)   *Silence = Agreement* where you assume that because no one raised any objections or aired concerns they must be in agreement.

I've found this approach is far better:

"Thanks for coming along to today's meeting. As you know, our target for this quarter is less than half way to being met and we only have three weeks to do something about it.

"I am sure that if we put our heads together we can use our combined experience to work out an effective plan of attack.

"I'd like to hear from each of you. I want to hear what you have to say. In your opinion what can we do starting right now that can get us back on track?"

I would list their suggestions for all to see, give credit and encouragement to those making them, weigh up each suggestion and after adding my own expertise devise a plan that would recognise achievement and provide reward.

Too many leaders think that because they are bosses they have to think up strategies all by themselves.

That is a great mistake. It shows a misunderstanding of modern management. No-one has a monopoly on good ideas. By excluding input from others you deprive yourself of their resourcefulness and experience. I know, because earlier in my management career that was one of my major failings.

A successful technique for ensuring that doubts and differing views are aired is to appoint a 'devil's advocate' whose job is to argue against the motion. This would lead to discussion and avoid another common weakness of meetings; *letting a few do all the talking.*

The role of a good leader is to point the way, then use every resource to co-ordinate the efforts of those in his charge to achieve a desired goal. The challenge is to lead others to lead themselves.

To do this we need co-operation. However the 'boss' also needs to co-operate. If this thought makes you feel insecure, it shouldn't because far more is achieved in a spirit of harmony and co-operation than in an atmosphere of disapproval or autocracy. Not the least of those achievements is a far happier staff - and boss.

Willing co-operation is an unmistakeable quality of Personal Excellence.

Summary

You will succeed more quickly and to a greater extent by working with others than by working on your own.

The principles discussed will help you achieve co-operation. However there is one ingredient which you and you alone can add; *A genuine empathy for the needs and aspirations of those around you.*

People will recognise the person who has a sincere regard for their welfare and who promotes a win-win outcome.

If you only remember one aspect of this section let it be this; before you act, put yourself in the mind of those you want to influence. Ask yourself;

"How would I feel? How would I like to be approached?"

Then proceed with Self leadership and Personal Excellence.

7

Influencing Yourself - Self-Motivation

Most of us would like the ability to influence other people and eagerly look for new ways to do so. But the key to influencing others is the ability to influence and lead ourselves. It comes back to looking out by looking in; to Self-leadership; to Personal Excellence.

Self motivation is not something you can turn on and off like a light bulb. It is a way of living; an outlook, an ability to draw out what is best in you and lead yourself into action.

Do you remember the story of the mother whose face was terribly disfigured by fire after she had rescued her daughter? She was self-motivated to risk her life because her reasons to succeed were sufficiently compelling.

Achievers don't wait for external events, threats of losing their job or for anything else to motivate them. They motivate themselves. They know that external motivation is only temporary; that it doesn't last.

What Motivates You?

Have you ever wondered, deep down, what motivates you? Take time to list those things which really get you going (e.g., recognition, prestige, family life, pressure, challenge, self-improvement, financial security, leisure time, personal growth, etc.)

Once you know what really motivates you, you can use that knowledge to:

- increase your success

- increase your happiness

- enjoy your work more

- win more respect

- like yourself and others even better

If this sounds like promising a miracle, it is! You are empowered to work miracles in your life. All you need are an understanding and acceptance of the self-motivation keys. To work for you they require application and Self leadership. Why not absorb the principles and apply them until they become a part of the way you live and work?

Self-motivation is money-making good.

A Dynamic Attitude

Often we cannot see what is right in front of our eyes because our attitude prevents it. Consider the following encounter between two new arrivals in town and an old man:

John:(To the old man)   *"We plan on stayin' here for awhile. Look for work. Can you tell me what people are like 'round here?"*

Old Man: *"What were the people like where you have come from?"*

John: *"Most unfriendly, cold, forbidding people I ever saw."*

Old Man: *"People around here are no different!"* he replied. Noting the flash of disappointment in Ted's eyes he asked him *"What are the people like in your home town?"*

Ted: *"Great! Warm, friendly, always speak kindly to strangers."*

Old Man: *"Pleased to hear it, because people here are no different!'*

If we go through life seeking negatives we find them in abundance. When we look for positives we find them in abundance too.

By projecting our own travelogue we'll keep finding the inevitable; people don't fit into our picture.

So why not seek the good? The positive? The motivational? They will help you achieve your Major Life Goal and strengthen Personal Excellence.

Do you see traffic lights as 'stop lights' or 'go lights?' Is a day partly cloudy, or partly sunny? Is the glass half empty, or half full? It's all in how you see things. Maintain a positive attitude and everything around you becomes positive too.

An Urge to Act, to Draw from Within, to Lead Oneself

Have your ever promised yourself; "I'll really do (X) as soon as (Y) happens?"

Any excuse to procrastinate, right?

I suspect God might blame us more for the things we haven't done than for those things we have done.

In the words of Psychologist Dr Susan Jeffers:

"Most of us do not 'sculpt' our lives. We accept what comes our way ..... then we gripe about it. Many of us spend our lives waiting - waiting for the perfect mate, waiting for the perfect job, waiting for perfect friends to come along. There is no need to wait for anyone to give you anything in your life. You have the power to create what you need. Given commitment, clear goals and action, it's just a matter of time."

(From 'Feel the Fear and Do it Anyway')

What often stops people from doing what they really want is their reluctance to endure any initial discomfort. Many of us are conditioned to relinquish a long term gain for an immediate reward.

But then you might ask; is anyone who is not prepared to back his own abilities by accepting risk, worthy of receiving the reward?

Whatever your answer, self-motivation depends on your following the storyline you have written for yourself and on your ability to draw out what is best in you.

Self-Motivation is Self-Leadership

Self leadership has four key disciplines:

- Practice

- Organisation

- Goals

- Energy

To succeed in self motivation you need to be an *activationist*. Practice your skills. Organise your day; week; month: year, future. Set goals good enough to excite you. Build a reputation for energy; for getting things done. Put in that extra effort. Life itself is action; movement.

Encourage yourself. Guide yourself. Praise yourself. Reinforce your positives. Focus on the rewards that come when the task is done not on the task itself. Lead yourself to that reward.

'Do it now!' Is the motto of the self-motivated.

$$S = \frac{Asl^2}{PE}$$

(Success formula refresher: *Success = Attitude times Self leadership squared over Personal Excellence*)

We Get 27,375 Chances (Days) to Win

Every day we get another chance to try again. For a person who lives to age 75, life will grant him some 27,375 chances.

Every day Life says; *"Here's another 24 hours. Try again."*

Me: *"But I've blown it. I've messed it up!'*

Life: *"Don't worry. Here's another 24 hours. Try again."*

Me: *"Sorry. I've goofed again."*

Life: *"That's OK. Here's another 24 hours. Take another shot. You can do it. Be a self-leader."*

For most of us Life does this day in, day out, 27,375 times.

Isn't that wonderful? Past mistakes don't count if you're willing to try again! Doesn't the very thought of it motivate you?

Our future is in our tomorrows. Thankfully, God gives us a new tomorrow every day.

What's the Point of Being Negative?

Being negative is obstacle thinking, not opportunity thinking. It is also far less practical. Research shows that only about 10% of what we worry about actually happens. So benefits aside, isn't being positive 90% more practical?

Negativity distorts our view of others, of ourselves and of the world around us! Why empower negative people, events or circumstances to drag us down? To throw rocks into our pond? Why cultivate a Martyr Mentality? Martyrs die.

In 'Super Leadership' Dr Charles C. Manz and Professor Henry P Sims write;

"Research shows that individual's expectations become self-fulfilling prophecies; that is, positive expectations enhance the probability of actually doing it. Conversely, negative expectations decrease the probability. The state of mind about oneself has a clear impact on ultimate performance."

Recently I met an old acquaintance window shopping. He was in his fifties, serene and very happy. This itself is not unusual. However I discovered that he suffered from an enzyme deficiency which caused his lungs to shrink. He was given eight years to live.

I couldn't work out how he could be so happy! But as he saw it, some people only had eight days.

Negativity is a disease fatal to success, but the cure is readily available.

When we know where we are heading and put on a positive mental attitude we get better straight away!

Everyone gets better after we do.

You might be thinking . . . *"But I've got problems!"*

Congratulations! That's great! Life is all about solving problems. The only people without problems are dead.

A problem is an invitation to us to grow; to succeed.

Problems themselves cannot beat us. It is the way we see them and what we do about them that counts.

Negativity never solved a problem but created many! If you say you have enough problems why create more by being negative?

Consider the following true story:

A Minister of the Church was struggling to write his sermon because Tim, his nine year old son, kept interrupting.

Finally he hit on an idea. He remembered seeing a map of the world printed on a travel brochure he kept in his drawer. He quickly tore the page into two dozen small pieces and promised Tim that if he could put all the pieces back in the right order, he would buy him all the ice cream he could eat.

The minister was certain Tim would be kept busy for hours, but to his dismay, not 10 minutes had elapsed before Tim proudly announced he had completed the puzzle.

"How did you do it?", asked the minister.

Tim replied; *"There is a picture of a person on the back. I knew that if I got the person right, the world would be right.*

Convert Dissatisfaction Into Motivation

There are two types of dissatisfaction; proactive and reactive.

You can recognise reactive dissatisfaction any time you hear someone whine or complain. Those people love misery. They have heaps of it and want to share it with everyone. They have the mentality of the Martyr.

Reactive dissatisfaction is the way of the low achiever.

Proactive dissatisfaction is *a force for good*. It is powerful. It creates energy. It gives a sense of direction and achievement. It's money-making good.

This true story of a 12 year old boy's experience illustrates the power of proactive dissatisfaction:

David O'Connell lived in a country town of about 50,000 people in Queensland, Australia.

For a whole year he worked after school at odd jobs and saved every cent until he had the money he needed to buy his very own bicycle.

The Saturday before Christmas was the most important day of his life. David gave the money to his father who promised to buy the bicycle and bring it home.

The bicycle never arrived. David's father had called into a hotel and spent the money on drink. His father was an alcoholic.

David had enough reactive dissatisfaction to last a lifetime. But he was too bright and proud to let a temporary setback rob him of his dream.

For a month he let proactive dissatisfaction work for him. He led himself to the local tip and found a bicycle frame in good repair.

He scrounged and borrowed, traded and pleaded until he got a wheel here, a handle-bar there and every part he needed to build his own bicycle.

David is a successful financial planner. His eyes still sparkle when he tells the story of how at the age of 12 he built his own bicycle: *"The best and fastest in town."*

Recognising proactive dissatisfaction is simple. It embodies a specific promise to solve the problem, such as:

"I'm fed up with being broke! I'm sick and tired of not being able to provide the lifestyle my family deserves. Starting right now, I'm going to strive for success. I'm going to learn all there is to know about succeeding. I'm going to succeed if it takes every ounce of my strength and I'm going to do it with integrity."

See the difference? Proactive dissatisfaction becomes a catalyst for action. It is the power behind humankind's great achievements because the achievers were dissatisfied in a proactive way.

The discoveries of medical science had their origins in proactive dissatisfaction with suffering and disease.

Proactive dissatisfaction is your subconscious telling you that you can do better.

Keep a Bank of Positive Thoughts

How often do we read a phrase that 'speaks to us' but subsequently forget it?

It is useful to keep a notebook indexed A to Z. Whenever you read a quote, phrase or idea which is meaningful for you, jot it down.

It also works as an energy charger for self-motivation. By reading through your notes from time to time you will refresh your spirit, redirect your thinking and put that spring back into your step.

Motivate Someone Else Every Day

A phone call, card, letter, flower or other thought can really brighten someone's day, especially when given with sincere appreciation.

Here again, the law of increasing returns applies. By giving motivation to others you'll get it back a hundredfold. You will receive motivation in return plus the pleasure of knowing you have brightened someone's day.

In a recent position I had three secretaries working with me. Sometimes the pressure of their work combined with personal and work-related squabbles increased tension in the office. I was always amazed how a little thought or gesture of appreciation swept away days of friction.

The thought? I would buy each of them a small chocolate; or a cake for morning coffee, or take them out for a cappuccino. Nothing elaborate, just some little thing to show them they were appreciated and that I valued them as people as well as employees. This worked even by remote control. A humorous card or phonecall would often do the trick.

I did this even for our Head Office staff when I knew of a section which was under extraordinary pressure. One time I sent a bouquet of flowers with a message of appreciation for all their past work to three different sections. The reaction was electric. No one had done that before.

The notes of thanks, phonecalls, handshakes and kisses I received was far more gratifying to me than the cost of my small gesture ever merited. From that day on, any work sent to Head Office from my Region was processed swiftly, efficiently and cheerfully.

And the result in my own Region? Dedication and loyalty. Many extra hours worked without reward and without having to be asked.

Why did I do it? The answer is ; out of *pure selfishness*. It gave me a great feeling to see the appreciation in their eyes. I enjoyed making people feel good about themselves, and I wanted more of it. But above all, *it motivated me more than it did them.*

If You Can't Change it, Cool it

The spectacle of an impatient, fuming driver stuck in a traffic jam is a common example of mild dementia. How does it help to get out and shout; "Come on! Move it!"?

What is the point of raising your stress level if the event has already happened and you can't do anything about it?

Surely only fools worry about what they can't change or control?

After all, events are of two kinds: those that concern you and which you can influence, and those that concern you but which you can't influence.

Why empower the *can'ts* to frustrate you and drag you down? Of themselves they are merely events. It is you who choose to give them power to hurt you. So the next time someone does something to displease you, remember that it has already been done. You can't rearrange it so it didn't really happen.

The best advice I know on 'cooling it' is this: "If something's happened that you don't like, if you can change it, go ahead and do it. If it's something you can't change, then all the worry and fuss in the world won't make the slightest difference. So what's the good of worrying and fussing over things you can't do anything about?"

Even for those who achieved outstanding success, neither people nor life were prepared to fit precisely into their plans. Yet they succeeded in crying "Enough!" In changing their life forever; in success through Self leadership and Personal Excellence.

Why empower other people or events to cancel your day? Or to cancel your future? It's not your fault that God didn't see fit to distribute intelligence in equal measure. You can curse those who frustrate you all you like, but they probably don't even know you exist.

Happiness is in the Way You Think

George Bernard Shaw had a marvellous way of looking at joy. He wrote;

"This is the true joy in life - that of being used for a purpose recognised by yourself as a mighty one; being a force of nature, instead of a feverish, selfish little clod of ailments and grievances complaining that the world will not devote itself to making you happy. I am of the opinion that my life belongs to the whole community and as long as I live it is my privilege to do for it whatever I can. I want to be thoroughly used up when I die. For the harder I work the more I live. I rejoice in life for its own sake. Life is no brief candle for me. It's a sort of splendid torch which I've got to hold up for the moment and I want to make it burn as brightly as possible before handing it on to future generations".

Happiness or unhappiness is largely a state of mind. This is not surprising when you consider that life itself is mostly thought, not form. You can test this easily. Stretch out your hand and snatch a moment of life.

Now open your hand.

How did you go?

Just like the rest of us mortals!

As things happen they instantly pass into time. Think of an event that happened last week. Where is it now? Does it exist?

Viewed correctly this is a most wonderful discovery for happiness. If life is mostly thought, then we can be as happy as we make up our minds to be because we control our thoughts!

We need not wait until we win the lottery, drive the latest sports car or live in a bigger house by a lake. These are form, not thought. Every piece of form we own will be serving someone else a few years from now!

To be happy or unhappy *is a matter of choice* because happiness comes from within ourselves.

To quote Stephen R Covey;

"I have had the opportunity to work with many people - wonderful people, talented people who want to achieve happiness and success, people who are searching, people who are hurting. I've worked with business executives, college students, church and civic groups, families and marriage partners. And in all my experience, I have never seen lasting solutions to problems, lasting happiness and success, that came from the outside in."

(From 'The Seven Habits of Highly Effective People')

Rinse Your Brain

Have you ever met a pukeaholic? He's the master of 'stinkin' thinkin'; of striving to be average, of living life by the Law of Accident.

A pukeaholic is the person who can't resist 'throwing up' his woes all over you. Ask him how he is - and he'll tell you! He'll add the traffic jam on the way to work, the row with his wife, the high cost of living, difficult customers, ingrown toenails - the lot.

Suddenly, puke! puke! puke!

Who needs it?

Pukeaholics are also people in the process of becoming 'if only's', or 'I could have beens'

The thing about puking problems onto others is that half of them don't care you have them, and the other half are glad!

Get Excited About Your Major Life Goal

One of the greatest self-motivators is to recommit yourself frequently to achieving your Major Life Goal; that's why it's vital to write it down.

Without the sense of purpose and direction provided by a Major Life Goal and the solid foundation embodied in your personal

Totem it is almost certain you can't live a happy, motivated and successful lifestyle.

You will, of course, be motivated by external events from time to time. But these 'highs' serve only to punctuate the despair of your 'lows'. Once the high is gone you start to wander again, blown adrift by every wind of change.

There are few feelings as motivating as those which help you see you're going where you want to go.

If you haven't determined your Major Life Goal I urge you to do it now. You will experience great satisfaction when you have written it down and committed to its achievement through Self leadership and Personal Excellence.

Your Personal Interpreter

Few would say they engage a personal interpreter, yet everybody has one.

I am talking about that indispensable of self-motivation: a Positive Mental Attitude (PMA). When you have P.M.A. it acts as a wonderful interpreter. For example, during the early days of World War One, Ferdinand Foch, Marshal of France, was asked how things were going on his front.

He replied; *"My right wing is in retreat. My left wing is withdrawing. My centre is disintegrating. Situation excellent. I am attacking!"*

Your interpreter will tell you that:

- Cost is investment.

- A problem is a challenge.

- A mistake is a chance to try again more intelligently.

- A setback is a road sign to be read before proceeding.

- 'Failure' is success deferred, not denied.

P.M.A. creates a bright atmosphere of hope. It switches you onto the success wavelength. It interprets everyday occurrences into a sparkling language that transforms defeat into victory.

Your P.M.A. interpreter; *don't leave home without it.*

Inoculate Against Excusitis

Every low achiever has this disease in its advanced form. People afflicted with excusitis can give you a litany of excuses. They all have a 'wooden leg' and seldom list themselves as the chief reason for not achieving.

They invent more excuses than they need in case they don't have a strong enough case to fail!

George Bernard Shaw hated excuses. He wrote:

"People are always blaming their circumstances for what they are. I don't believe in circumstances. The people who get on in this world are the people who get up and look for the circumstances they want, and, if they can't find them, make them."

Defeat Fear of Failure/Rejection/Success

As has been seen in 'Attitude Barriers', many people are conditioned into fear from a very early age. However in its strict biological sense fear is a primitive urge for survival. It prepares us to run or fight.

If you choose fear (to run) it will obey you by generating negative feelings. If you choose to fight (persistence) your subconscious helps you by generating positive feelings. Then you look for ways to win!

The answer is in the choice you make.

Substitute feelings of fear with positive feelings by keeping your mind on future successes; on the things you want and off the things you don't want.

Aim High

Life is an obedient employer. It will pay only the wages you demand of it! The higher you aim the more you will achieve.

Satisfied needs don't motivate. You won't achieve Personal Excellence by aiming at mediocrity.

Enthusiasm

Enthusiasm without action is of little value. Combined with correct action enthusiasm alone can double your success.

If you're not enthused about yourself, your company, your job, your product, why are you there?

The great John Wesley, founder of the Methodist Church, was forbidden to preach in the churches of his day. He had to preach in the street or in fields. Yet he attracted thousands of people to his sermons whilst mainstream churches were relatively empty. Asked how he could draw so many people he replied; *"I set John Wesley on fire, and they come to watch me burn."*

When was the last time you 'set yourself on fire' with enthusiasm?

When my enthusiasm is running low I take a few days off and step back from what I've been doing so I can see the wider picture. As part of this strategy I always visit a resort, well-to-do estate or affluent tourist area and enjoy the view of expensive yachts bobbing up and down on a glassy marina, the multi-million dollar homes, the sculptured lawns and gardens, the private clubs, the up-market boutiques, restaurants, cafes, etc.

I find that surrounding myself with those visual promises has a positive effect on my motivation. It reminds me that it is all possible; that people can live with comfort and dignity if they are prepared to work and struggle to achieve their dream.

It is not the display of wealth that I find motivating. It is the strong sense that a life of dignity, of freedom from want, puts us right up there where we all belong.

8

Your Moments of Truth

Leonard Bernstein faced his moment of truth when Bruno Zirato phoned him in the dark hours of morning and said;

"Well, this is it. You have to conduct at 3 o'clock this afternoon. No chance for a rehearsal. There is no way to get the orchestra together and you will report at a quarter to three backstage at Carnegie Hall and conduct this afternoon."

This was the first time he was to conduct a major philharmonic orchestra. What if Leonard Bernstein had not studied and practiced all those years?

What did he do in his moment of truth? In his own words;

"So there I am, standing in the wings. All atremble.... listening to Bruno Zirato who had come out on stage to address the audience and tell them the unhappy news that they would not be hearing Bruno Walter that day. Many groans. But instead they would be hearing a young conductor called Leonard Bernstein, the assistant conductor of the Philharmonic, and on I had to come .... I strode out and that's the last thing I remember until the end of the concert when I saw the entire audience there, standing and cheering and screaming."

(From 'Leonard Bernstein' by Joan Peyser)

And so a brilliant career was launched. Leonard Bernstein faced his moment of truth, and triumphed.

Most of us face moments of truth of one sort or another every day.

Elvis Presley had to decide whether he really wanted to be a singer when after his first concert he was told he should consider becoming a truckdriver. Composers Handel, Schumann, Bernstein, Varese and Boulez had fathers who were strongly against their chosen vocation, yet persisted. (Varese's father locked the piano, covered it with a shroud and threw away the key). When leading fashion designer Elsa Schiaparelli looked for design work she was told she would be better off planting potatoes!

These moments test our resolve; our Self leadership. They are moments which test our effectiveness through the way we respond to people and to our job.

It's all very well to base your success journey on a road of integrity and principle (Personal Excellence). But how do you respond when your principles are challenged?

What would you have done if you were the advertising executive who was instructed to create a campaign which would hook adolescents onto smoking? That executive wept; but he did it anyway.

If you could make money out of a 'slightly shady' deal and knew you wouldn't get caught, would you do it?

Would you overlook the transgressions of a key employee if he were a valued performer?

When General Manager of a large holiday resort development I had to dismiss my sales manager and a key employee. It was a decision which really hurt because, their value aside, I was particularly fond of the sales manager.

Unfortunately he was engaged in an affair with one of his subordinates and the situation was undermining the morale of other staff. Accusations of favourite treatment, gossip, loss of respect - especially as it broke up his marriage - had eroded the goodwill that all members of his team had for him.

Initially I didn't want to believe it was happening, hoping it would go away. But eventually I had to move, and did. I must say the organization was better for the example, although even years later I still wish there had been some way of keeping him and retaining our friendship.

It was a moment of truth that wouldn't go away.

Success through Personal Excellence also requires us to be consistent, and as discovered by the armed services, this can only come through preparation and practice.

Of course, we must be honest with ourselves and recognise our own limitations. As a wise man once put it: *"I'm smart in spots so I stay around those spots."*

We can study a dozen success courses, nod wisely, agree and become enthused only to let it unravel as soon as we are faced with the principal requirement; effort. (For example have you written your personal Totem as suggested earlier? Have you determined your core values? Have you decided on the success you want for each sphere of life?) Your answers to those questions might help you see the truth in the wholistic success formula:

$$\frac{S = Asl^2}{PE}$$

Moments of truth arise whenever our commitment is tested.

Australian swimming coach Laurie Lawrence showed his commitment in a startling way. When a swimmer complained of pain in pushing himself for one more lap of the pool;

"That's not pain!" he replied, scraping his clenched fist against a rough-brick wall. Holding up his bleeding knuckles he said; *"That's pain! Now get on with it!"*

Is it any wonder he trains Olympic champions?

I faced a personal moment of truth when operating my own Public Relations and Marketing consultancy. The business was in its infancy and I needed all the clients I could get. Two lucrative offers came my way. The first was a promotion contract with a major cigarette company, and the other was a similar contract with a leading brewery.

The money I could have made would have saved me several years of struggle. However I had to face my own principles, which are that I will not help promote any tobacco products, nor will I help promote alcohol. Please don't form the impression that I want to stop people having a drink. I simply will not do anything to encourage anyone to drink more than they do already, or to harm their health - and that of others - by smoking.

The result? Someone else filled the gap. But that's fine because it wasn't me. In the long run the decision freed up time for me to accept a consultancy with the Government of Western Australia, and another to promote a State-wide festival for a community-based group. Those appointments gave me far more credibility than I would have gained through the promotions I had turned down.

I faced another moment of truth when operating a travel agency and travel club. My partner was, at that time, the second largest travel wholesaler in Australia with offices in several countries.

Through my travel club we provided passengers for package holidays. However six months later my partner was placed in receivership, leaving many travellers with worthless tickets.

The moment of truth was: do I walk away from those passengers and suggest they put their loss down to experience? (I had no *legal* obligation to refund their money.) or do I make good their loss through personal savings because *there was a moral principle* involved?

I chose the latter, and although it sapped me of all my financial resources, years later I am still convinced it was one of the best decisions I've made.

Those were moments of truth challenging my personal Totem. There are many other kinds.

The following items are worth exploring because we need to become as skilled in handling moments of truth as the soldier is skilled in handling firearms.

Effort

Write down the amount of effort you are
putting into your work; (e.g. 25% 50% 75%) ___________

Write down the yearly income this amount
of effort is producing (e.g. 50% effort =
$xyz per year) $ ___________

Consider this formula carefully. Say you have
50% more effort to give, to what extent
would giving it; increase your income? $ ___________
increase your chances for promotion
(out of 100%)   _________% or
build your business? (out of 100%)   _________%

If by increasing your effort you will improve in any of those
areas write down your answer to the following three questions;

Do you want to earn more income?

Answer: ___________

Will using the energy you are holding back
help to do this for you?

Answer: ___________

What is stopping you?

Answer: ___________

If you want 100% success it will demand 100% effort.

Is there such a thing as 50% success? Few have succeeded on
50% effort and of successful people fewer still would agree
there is such a thing as half success.

Christian Dior was a task master who often made impossible
demands on staff at the last possible moment. Even after
working 18 hour days for weeks, an exhausted young tailor was
always first to volunteer for extra duties; his name? Pierre
Cardin.

Most people who give 100% effort usually love what they do. This also applies to sport (they love to win).

Some people who hold back on giving their 'all' do so because they are perpetual 'grazers'.

If you have interviewed people for senior positions you will have seen many resumes. You will have noticed many talented people who have achieved responsible positions in a variety of industries.

Moving from industry to industry can be a good thing for variety and experience. However the point has to come when the success-minded achiever has to stop 'grazing' if he is to attain his Major Life Goal.

You have to reach the watershed where you can say; *"This is me. I'm a banker. I'm a travel agent. I'm a salesperson. I will stop grazing and build my success here. I will resist any side-ways movement away from my chosen field. Here is where I will make my fortune. Here I stand."*

Until this point is reached, it is unlikely you will give 100% of your talent and abilities. How can you? You're still looking around in case you miss something.

Perpetual grazing is all right for those who are content to be one of the herd.

If you are giving less than 100% to your occupation perhaps you don't love what you do?

If you are going to share 8-10 hours of your day five or six days per week with an employer or in a business doing something you don't love, what's the point of doing it at all?

If you do not love what you do for a living decide what it is you really want, then do it. Make sure it will move you closer to your Major Life Goal. Stop grazing.

Obviously, you might not be able to change jobs straight away. You might need the work. That's now. What you can do is decide what it is you really want and prepare for a change, even if that change lies in the future.

Facing your moments of truth is not always a pleasant task. For example, do you like to run away from difficult situations or stick it out until they are resolved? Do you think of quitting your job every time something doesn't go your way? Can you organise and run a meeting? Can you manage people in a spirit of co-operation and harmony?

Skill

What is your level of skill? Can you write a clear, concise letter? Do you manage the family budget so the money is set aside to meet regular bills such as rates, phone, electricity, etc., or do you panic every time you receive an account?

How good are you at problem-solving? The formula is simple enough:

- Ask: What is the problem? Write it down. What's happening or not happening?

- List the possible reasons for it. Are there facts to support your conclusions? Do you need more information before you can act?

- Whom do you need to consult?

- List possible solutions, then pick the best, taking people issues, risks, timing and economy of effort into account.

- Decide on the solution and on methods for its application. Apply your solution. Evaluate its effectiveness.

- Throughout this procedure, keep re-stating the problem. (You'll be surprised how often you catch yourself in the process of solving the wrong problem!)

Sometimes the way we see the problem, is the problem.

Personal Quality Control

Quality control in manufacturing checks not only the quality of materials but the manufacturing process itself, including products.

If you were to break your job down to a series of steps and someone checked each step randomly, would you be happy with the result?

We are paid for quality time; for quality results we bring to an organisation. Was your answer on the amount of effort you are putting into your work 100%?

If it was only 50% you could owe your organisation half your wages!

Divide your work into steps and apply your own quality control. Check each step to ensure it is done as well as you are able. Determine to succeed. Accept this as your first moment of truth.

Believe in quality. Push for quality. Achieve quality.

The father of mass production was Eli Whitney (inventor of the cotton gin and the mass-produced rifle). He staggered competitors with low-cost, high-quality armaments. The secret was a line of workers each responsible for manufacturing various pieces of a rifle. Up until then, each rifle was made completely by one person.

His secret was quality. Each piece had to be made with a high degree of precision so it would fit into another piece made by someone else, and so on.

Henry Ford used this principle in manufacturing his Model T.

Mass production (speed) is made possible by ensuring quality in each step of the process. It depends on quality work.

Self-led is much more effective than externally-led quality control because in the former method, Self leadership is involved.

Traditional Japanese see inanimate objects almost as if they have an inherent life or soul. Japanese craftsmen and workers take great pride in what they produce.

Thomas J Peters and Robert H Waterman Jr., in their work, 'In Search of Excellence' tell the story of a Honda employee who on his way home would straighten the wiper blades on any Honda he would see parked nearby. He could not bear to see a flaw in something he had made.

To get a feeling for this philosophy of pride, try an experiment. Pick up any manufactured item and focus on it. Imagine it as if it were a thing of great inherent value. How could it be improved? What changes would you recommend? What flaws have been built into it through lack of pride?

Let quality be your label.

The beginning of success is the place where you are employed. Do your job much better. Do it fantastically better. Build a reputation for energy, skill, co-operation, honour and quality! Do your job so well they couldn't bear to lose you. Take charge. Be a strong leader of self.

Even if you plan to leave your job later become outstanding in it now. Leave it from a position of success; of strength; of Personal Excellence, not weakness. Let every company you ever work for be sorry to lose you. (Later you might want to buy the company!)

Are You a Morale Saboteur?

Do you like to air all the company's shortcomings? Whenever you don't agree with an issue, do you like to tell everyone about it? Do you like to huff and puff about people you don't like?

The answer is simple. Whenever you feel like talking to so and so about him or her; don't! If you don't like the company's decisions, don't puke your bile over others; leave. (A better solution would be to work your way up to a level where you can make the decisions you like.)

Active puking (you doing the puking) or passive puking (you doing the listening) is another version of 'wooden leg'. The only thing it achieves is to make others happier when you're not around.

Do You Have the Habit of Saving and Investing?

It is the money you save (and invest) which makes you wealthy, not the money you earn.

You can test this rule quite simply. Can you write a cheque for $10,000 and honour it? If you had saved 20% of what you have earned to date, would that make a difference to your circumstances now?

(This area is so vital to success it forms a separate chapter. However it needs to be mentioned here as a moment of truth because we face this moment every payday.)

Management of Self

Where is the joy of wealth without health? The idea of obtaining wealth is to help us enjoy life! Yet so many fail when facing a moment of truth vital to their well-being.

Here are five key areas which help maintain quality of life;

Diet and Exercise

This has already been addressed earlier in the course. Your moment of truth is: What have you done about it today?

Research in England lists ninety-year-olds who do aerobics. Within a few weeks they increase their muscle tone and strength by a third. People are abandoning their wheelchairs and putting away their walking sticks.

There's no need to run a marathon or pump weights. A moderate exercise programme - even as little as 30 minutes three times per week - can keep you aerobically fit.

For what it's worth, I try to build some exercise into my daily routine. For example, I park as far as I can from where I want to go to force me to walk. I go on a brisk walk every day. I walk up stairs wherever possible. Those are only little things, but they add up.

Use it or lose it is the principle most apt to exercise. It's not good enough to 'conquer the great indoors'. You've got to move.

As for diet, one of the great crimes of Western Society is to spend billions of dollars convincing women in particular that they are the wrong shape. Why? So merchants can sell clothes, diets, fads, gym membership, books and so on. All the promoters of 'the message' have achieved is to make the majority of women unhappy with who they are, increase disorders such as anorexia nervosa and bulimia - and make vendors and publishers wealthier in the process.

To see the nonsense in their 'message' all it takes is a good look at people. Can you see the variety of shapes that makes up the human race? Those are real people. They are not air-brushed or stretched photographs of lanky 13 to 14 year olds destined to appear as older people in fashion magazines.

And what started this unnatural fuss? To the best of my knowledge it was to please couturiers who decided that their creations looked better on taller, slimmer people. So they put in their order for people to suit their fashions.

The price many women have had to pay is lower self esteem, a lifetime of 'watching their figure', spinal problems due to wearing high heels, and general dissatisfaction with who they are.

So when I mention diet, I am not talking of crash-diets, slimming diets or any other sure-fire weight loss programme. I mention it in the context of a balanced, nutritious intake of food designed to give you energy, not take it from you.

Leadership of self also means management of self in diet and exercise. It also means self-acceptance.

Managing Stress

Laughter and sex are the two greatest stress relievers we know. However as the Director of the Coolum Hyatt Resort, Dr John Tickell, says; *"If they come together you know you're getting old."*

Externally we encounter pressure. Stress is something we create internally. It can be a good or bad thing, depending on how you see it and what you do about it. If you like the stress of challenge and you use this to achieve a good result, that's great!

If you see stressful situations as overwhelming and unpleasant then you will have a negative reaction to stress and could weaken your immune system. You could develop stress-related problems ranging from heart disease to itching.

Those with a positive mental attitude see challenging situations as opportunities. This is a good use of stress. Achieving and winning are good for us. They have physical and psychological benefits.

However we need to build in safety valves. In other words, we need to unwind regularly; to get out of the 'pressure-cooker' from time to time. We can do this through moderate exercise, mini vacations and a sensible diet.

Above all, we can help any stressful situation by maintaining a positive and cheerful outlook on life.

What happens when most people are confronted with a problem? They approach it full of stress and seriousness; losing their sense of balance and more often than not, they overreact.

Imagine tackling the same problem after a belly laugh or joyful experience. Would not our approach change? We would not take ourselves so seriously and probably would solve the problem much more fairly and with a great deal less stress.

Why not develop a de-stressing routine to practice before and after a tense 'moment of truth'? This could be as simple as a three-minute relaxation exercise or a brisk walk.

Humour

The impact humour makes on our health is well documented. As has been said, happy, smiling people tend to be healthier, live longer, are more successful at life and raise happier children. This is not a 'modern' secret. Proverb 17.22 of The Jerusalem Bible teaches that:

"A glad heart is as an excellent medicine. A depressed spirit wastes the bones away."

A sense of humour is that ability to take our work seriously but ourselves lightly. It gives us perspective. It enables us to respond calmly and clearly in crises.

Sadly, as we grow older many of us lose our sense of humour; our sense of joy in living. C.W. Metcalf, a brilliant presenter, actor, mime and humorist, tells us we can develop a case of 'Terminal professionalism'. That is to say, we feel we have to be serious all the time; responsible; authoritative. We feel there must be something wrong with the person who laughs a lot and is joyful.

Our sense of humour, the ability to laugh at ourselves and take ourselves lightly actually boosts our immune system. Those who lose that ability suffer more, more often and longer than those who retain it.

C.W. Metcalf suggests the more 'humourless' among us should visit a private photo booth and take some pictures of ourselves pulling the funniest, most ridiculous face we know. When next we confront a tense situation we can take one of these photos out of our wallet and look at it!

Does that sound foolish?

It could be. However fear of 'foolishness' can prevent you from being spontaneous, happy, relaxed and joyful about living. Perhaps it is more foolish not to be 'foolish'?

Be unaffected; discard hangups. Be yourself! Enjoy life! As long as it doesn't hurt others, why not be a little 'foolish?'

Smoking

This drug has enslaved countless millions and lined the pockets of tobacco growers, manufacturers, advertisers, vendors and doctors alike.

We have already mentioned that cigarettes are the world's cheapest status symbol. In the words of a teenager: "When you go to a club or hotel, the first thing people want is to see you with a drink in one hand and a smoke in the other. It's as if having these things makes you a complete person'"

In tragic irony, the man who helped create the image of 'freshness, outdoors, etc.' by riding a horse through streams and open fields for cigarette advertisements died from lung cancer. Before his death he had become an ardent anti-smoking campaigner.

Did the cigarette companies get the message? Sadly, no. As smoking is declining in developed countries they have taken their wares to underdeveloped nations where strict advertising and other restrictions don't apply. The result? Smoking in those countries is on the increase.

Are you a smoker? Have you considered why you are injuring your health and paying someone else to do it?

Smoking can be an obstacle to achieving and maintaining Health. Your moment of truth is; give it up. Do it now. (Your health *and* wealth will improve straight away!)

Excessive Intake of Alcohol

What is excessive? It is difficult to drink moderately (a glass of wine with dinner, for example) when there is so much pressure in society to encourage drinkers to see themselves as 'macho' or as 'celebrities' if they drink to excess. However everyone can drink moderately if they are effective Self leaders.

Drinking to excess is the antithesis of Personal Excellence. You cannot be serious about wholistic success by saying; *"I'll achieve wealth but won't worry about health or Personal Excellence. "* Almost everyone is a role model to someone else.

Do you have more than two alcoholic drinks *every* day? Why not consider having at least three alcohol-free days per week? If that is difficult could it be because alcohol might have control of you rather than the other way around?

I believe it's a question worth asking.

Current General Knowledge

What do you know about economics? Recessions? Inflation? Interest Rates? etc. You need not be an economist to succeed. However a general understanding of economic cycles and trends would help enormously.

For example if the economic indicators are trending towards a deep recession you would be very cautious about the investments you make or the business you start.

If you don't have the knowledge, find out. Talk to someone who does. Read financial journals. Research before you act.

Other moments of truth face us whenever we need to solve a problem, make a decision, feel dispirited or lose our focus on where we are heading and why we want to get there (when we relinquish Self leadership and start to follow).

You won't be able to face your moments of truth consistently if you do not have a clear idea of who you are, what you stand for, where you want to go and why you need to get there. This knowledge is a filter for handling challenges. I helps you see what falls within your mission and what will lure you away from your Major Life Goal.

Recently I faced a moment of truth that will determine the outcome of the rest of my life. It was this; do I believe in my ability, in what I can contribute and achieve, or do I simply mouth platitudes and interesting stories from the comfort and security of a highly paid executive position?

If I believed in myself and my message then I shouldn't hesitate to throw in the job, the plush office, the company car with unlimited petrol, the bonuses and retirement package. I shouldn't equivocate about devoting the rest of my working life to practicing what I preach; to helping others achieve success through Self leadership and Personal Excellence.

The downside was my increasing age (only 45, but it's an age which begins to make you less attractive to many employers) and the fact that we were in the middle of Australia's worst ever recession.

Having faced this moment of truth the decision was simple: the storyline I wanted to live was the one I would write for myself. This book is one product of that commitment.

I could not have decided which way to go if I didn't have a clear idea of what I wanted, where I wanted to go and why I wanted to get there.

I discovered a long time ago that it's never enough to talk. One must also walk that talk.

9

Developing Your Instinct to Win-Win

The wonderful thing about winning is that after winning, there comes more winning. To enjoy our share we need to establish and practice winning behaviour patterns.

One essential behaviour pattern is to look at life as it is. This is not as easy as it might seem, especially if you have people around you who tell you of things as they would like you to see them.

Niccolo Machiavelli wrote a book titled 'The Prince'. It has gained a reputation as one of the most infamous literary works in history and he has even been compared with the devil.

Yet Machiavelli only sought to write a factual account of the realities of survival in the sixteenth century. He was telling his prince; *this is the set up. You don't have to like it, but if you want to survive you'd better know it.*"

Similarly in our own day, whilst we can strive for Personal Excellence by adopting a totem of honour and integrity for the sake of our happiness and the health of our community, it would be sheer folly to assume others will operate in the same way. The realities are that most people in business are constantly trying to gain an advantage by undermining their competitors. Advertising does it every day by trying to convince you that brand X is better than brand Y.

Do we really need to snatch our living from another man's throat? Do we need to become 'Machiavellian'? Is there reward for the businessman of character; the businessman of integrity?

Surprisingly, the answer is a firm "Yes!" Many of the world's great corporations were built on integrity. Nevertheless they hired lawyers to look over any contract before they signed it! In the words of former U.S. President Ronald Reagan, we need to: *"Trust, but verify."*

Let that be your first article of policy in developing your instinct to win-win.

The other 'reality' is that hard work alone does not guarantee you will be promoted or successful. Working diligently as one cog in a corporate wheel and hoping you'll be 'discovered' is not a particularly successful tactic.

The chances are that if your area is working smoothly (thanks to you), there is no fuss and you tow the company line, you probably won't even be noticed by those who count.

No one ever said we live in a fair and just world. Honesty and good are not always rewarded, neither is deceit and evil always punished. We might not like this reality but we have to know it.

The main thing is to live up to our Totem; to keep striving for wholistic success through Self leadership and Personal Excellence regardless of what others do.

Developing your instinct to win-win aims at spotlighting *success behaviour patterns* and ingraining these into your psyche; into your daily routine. These include:

Business is Business

Emotion is absolutely the worst basis for committing to a new business venture or for signing a contract. When you are in love with an idea, under pressure to grab that opportunity before it's too late or when people urge you to sign, that is a time to think, not blink.

In between jobs I was tempted to start a business with a partner who had a knack for promising much but delivering little. Nevertheless I had known him for many years and our dealings had always been satisfactory, so I took a plunge.

We worked together for several weeks, flew to Sydney to discuss contracts with lawyers, and generally began to organize our new venture. In the end, he went cold on the idea and wanted to reduce his financial involvement.

I responded by deciding to do the whole thing myself. I took the decision on an emotional basis just to prove it could be done. The result? I lost $30,000 in three months. But I learned that emotion and business seldom mix.

I also learned that in the marketplace no one gives medals for bravery.

I learned that whenever a business proposal is brought to us we need to consider it from a business perspective. We need to calculate the extent of cash receipts it is likely to produce either now or in the future. We need to ask; is the profit worth the effort? Will we accept a small loss now for a larger gain later? Is there a credit risk involved? What is the background of the proposer? If we are being urged to do it now, what's the hurry?

Don't be overawed by marble offices, chandeliers and carpets on the wall. If you are being urged to put your money into anything, check the people behind the scenes; their track record. Ask for other opinions and not necessarily those of a lawyer or accountant; they are good at what they do, but aren't necessarily good business people. Talk to someone who's felt the pain of financial loss.

Base your decision on business logic and your own sense of fair play. Remember that the market can only offer you money. If you are not making any, why are you there?

Should the proposal be a promotion to assist a charity, by all means decide on the nobler course if your cashflow can stand it.

On that point Peter S, a multi-millionaire developer from Perth, Australia says;

"I always look at any business deal in a detached loss and profit way. I never agree to a deal unless I'm sure it will add to the bottom line. Privately I would give you the shirt off my back. One's business, the other's private. That's the difference."

Business survival is about realism; about the way things are. Until you build sufficient assets to feel totally secure, view all your business dealings through the looking-glass of the bottom line. Once you have decided on a course, proceed with honour and integrity, with Personal Excellence. Nevertheless, trust but verify.

If in doubt about potential partners, why not follow Harvey Mackay's advice detailed in his book, 'Swim With The Sharks Without Being Eaten Alive.' He suggests; *"The second most important term (to add to a contract) is the right to inspect all their books and records, including tax records, etc., pertaining to the agreement. Once that clause is in there, people with a tendency to get cute usually don't."*

Hire People Smarter Than Yourself

You can't succeed without help from others so it's important to check references because good people are found, not made. Good people produce good work, bad people produce bad work. Ask yourself; *"If he were going to work for my competitor, would I feel threatened?"*

By hiring people who are smarter than yourself in their area of expertise, your company will grow. Hire those who are less smart and you will be fighting to keep your business from shrinking down to their size.

In the words of Harvey Mackay;

"Winners surround themselves with other winners. A winner knows he's a winner. He doesn't need second raters and yes-men around to feed his ego. He knows he'll win more, and

go further, with associates who not only can keep up with him but who are also capable of teaching him something. "

(From: How To Swim With The Sharks Without Being Eaten Alive)

People smarter than you will keep your instincts sharp, but only if you get out of their way. Don't give them a job only to take it away from them by telling them how they should do it.

However if you make a mistake, remember that often it's not the people you dismiss who can make your life a misery, but the people you keep.

You Can't be a Pal and a Boss

Business decisions need to be based on rational thinking and logic. They should not be influenced by personal feelings for people you like or dislike.

Bosses who try to win their employee's friendship often are despised for it.

That immortal Greek Slave, Aesop, tells the story of a fox who meets a lion for the first time. At first he is afraid of the lion and keeps his distance. The second time he is not so afraid, and walks a little closer. The third time he walks right past, ignoring the lion completely. The moral Aesop gives is that *"Familiarity breeds contempt. "*

Promoting Fast: Self-Promotion

When an attractive career change is offered by your corporation you might have to decide on transfer to another State (or Country).

If you want to promote fast you need to be prepared to move geographically as well as vertically.

If you are prepared to move, make sure the right people know about it.

As has been said, working hard won't, of itself, move you up the corporate ladder. You might not even be noticed.

To promote fast you're got to promote yourself by letting people see what you can do.

Be a strong self-leader. Go the extra mile. Think of ways to improve your job; to improve practices in other sections. Research them, put in suggestions with copies to the right people. Show you are thinking beyond your brief; beyond today. Show interest in what your company does. Volunteer. Always put top quality into your submissions, including evidence that you have thought things through such as listing consequences of your recommendations.

You can 'promote' yourself as easily as writing to a person to thank them for a job interview. How many people do that? Whose resume will they remember more readily?

Playing the 'Game'

If you were a member of a football team you would strive to win. You would tackle hard, risk pain, run like hell and break through to a goal.

Your opposition wants to do the same thing. Like you, they have a determined will to win. They train for it. Get in their way and they'll knock you down. Head for a goal and they'll do everything to stop you.

There is nothing personal in this. It's all part of the game. The important thing is to go for a win (which may contradict what you might have been taught at Sunday school).

Yet off the field you wouldn't dream of tackling an opposing player. The action would be irrelevant and out of context.

Business is very much like that. At work you're tackling, running, pushing and striving to kick goals (ensuring every deal is profitable). Privately you can invite your competitors to dinner.

When you 'go to work' you step onto the 'playing field' and you do that to win.

You can develop your instinct to win by putting on your 'Player's hat' whenever you walk into your office.

As for any player, you are a hero only when you win. Lose, and you get sympathy - sometimes. When you lose in business you can get bankruptcy.

If you feel strongly about winning, remember that the person you are up against probably feels the same way. Therefore there cannot be a winner at all unless both are satisfied with an outcome; unless both win in some way.

The secret of developing your instinct to win-win is the one used by football teams; training, training and practice.

In their book, 'Super Leadership', Dr Charles C Manz and Professor Henry P Sims Jr write;

"A recent study of many of our nation's (USA) top artists, scholars and athletes indicated their success resulted more from determination and practice than from natural, inborn talent.

"They had been encouraged early on to value hard work and to be inquisitive learners, and over time they blossomed into great performers."

$$\underline{S = Asl^2}$$

PE

(Success formula refresher: *Success equals Attitude times Self leadership squared over Personal Excellence.*)

Practice is preparation. When correct preparation meets opportunity (i.e., your moments of truth, a business proposal, a sales call) the result most often is success!

The Warm-up Before the Event

Athletes warm up before a game. They warm up physically, emotionally and mentally. They think through their strategy, visualise success and work to their game plan.

Many business leaders, top flight salespeople and entrepreneurs adopt the same 'warm up' strategy before conducting a business deal, staff meeting or sales call.

David R., the top sales representative for a large insurance company plays each call on the 'movie-screen' in his mind before he meets a client. He imagines the interview, what he will say, the client's response, what he will reply, and most often it results in a 'sale'.

Through his system he is able to approach the call with positive expectations and total confidence.

This confidence influences the client and helps establish trust. The result? David R not only enjoys a very high income and the respect of his colleagues, but the respect and recommendation of his clients as well!

What do you do to 'warm up' before each 'game'?

Become Your Own University

Despite how good you are to people or how much they like you, in the end none of them will pay your overdraft or rent. You are the only person on whom you can rely totally.

Develop your own philosophy and personal Totem by which to live. Increase your bank of knowledge. Update.

Would you be confident about an operation if you knew that your surgeon had been trained forty years ago and had not updated his knowledge?

The better your knowledge, the better your decisions. Read. Talk. Listen. Get ideas. Write them down.

Learn from your own experiences, from the experience of others, from books, tapes and videos. Learn from failure as well as success. Observe.

Authors regard libraries as their second office. That's where they get ideas and background material (i.e. knowledge). Why not learn from their example?

By changing your thinking you can change your life.

Sharpen your instinct to win-win by making self-education one of your major goals and a life-long endeavour.

English painter John Turner had himself tied to a ship's mast in foul weather so later he could paint the full onslaught of a storm!

Become a serious scholar

Buy an A to Z indexed 'Success Journal'. Take it with you to work, to seminars and meetings. Keep it with you whenever you're travelling. Have it beside you when you read. Record all your good ideas; good ideas from others, your experiences.

It might only cost you a trifling but what will it be worth when you have filled it? Why not let your completed success journals take pride of place in your personal success library?

Let them form the core of your self-education and self-development resources. By the time you retire, what a treasure of thoughts and experiences you will have to pass on to your children!

The urge to win is the same as the urge to know. You've just got to!

Getting the Numbers Right With Self Leadership

Out of one hundred per cent, how well do you score in the following key success areas?

Regular Saving and Investment(10%?)   __________%

Daily reading(0%?)   __________%

Being faithful to your personal Totem(0%?) _________%

Self leadership(30%?) _________%

Goal Setting(0%?) _________%

Personal Excellence(0%?) _________%

Steering towards your specific
Major Life Goal(0%?) _________%

Associating with winners(0%?) _________%

Out of a possible total of 800%? _________%

If the printed scores are anything like yours, the problem is not with the government, taxes, your mother-in-law or the weather; it's with your low scores!!

With self-leadership you can increase your scores straight away and begin to change your life immediately.

This is how easy it can be:

Score

Savings. Let a part of what you earn be yours to keep
and invest (10% to 20% each week)   100%

Read success books, know-how-to books and skill
books daily   100%

Be faithful to your Totem   100%

Lead yourself to improve your work habits
(give your best instead of holding back)   100%

Set short and long term goals; design your future for
the next ten years, for retirement and beyond   100%

Commit to a *specific* Major Life Goal;
write it down   100%

Achieve your Major Life Goal a minor goal at a time
through Self leadership and Personal Excellence   100%

Disassociate with low-achievers; mix with winners
(Ask; who am I mixing with? What am I letting them
do to me? What have they got me reading, thinking?
What have they got me becoming?   100%

Total score: 800%

Even if you only improve by 30% you will have increased your chances for success by at least that much! All you need is Self leadership.

Famous French author Victor Hugo found the Self leadership to write each day, difficult. But he knew it was vital, so he ordered his servants to steal all his clothes in the morning so he couldn't go out.

John Bunyan wrote his classic; 'The Pilgrim's Progress' while he was serving a 12 year sentence for preaching without a licence. Self leadership made the difference.

Admiral Nelson, Britain's great naval hero, suffered from severe sea-sickness all his life. Self leadership enabled him to cope.

In 1990 the Dachau Symphony Orchestra comprised 16 musicians of the original 65. The 16 who survived the horrors of the concentration camps played for the people in Dachau. They refused to empower the brutality around them to rob them of their dignity and the dignity of their fellow victims.

Self leadership; Personal Excellence; the unmistakable qualities of true winning.

It's pointless mouthing motivational phrases, affirming to yourself that you're positive, improving, etc., if you cannot lead yourself. Without Self leadership self-motivation leads to disillusionment.

For example, controlling emotions when something goes wrong is very important. You'll think far more creatively and clearly. But it takes Self leadership to do it.

We can't help how we feel but we can help what we do about it.

Here's a moment of truth. See how strong you are as a self-leader. If you smoke; stop! If you are excessively overweight; reduce! If you don't exercise regularly; do so! If you hold back at work; give all you've got!

Set yourself a goal of 14 days. *Just 14 days!* In any one of those areas.

If you don't have the Self leadership to achieve in those areas, where will you get it to persist in the tough make-or-break world of business? Of corporate reality? I have said all along that success takes effort. It demands effort. A self-led effort to keep us from having to pay the price of failure.

We can all draw inspiration from the most self-led species on Earth; the ant.

The ant heads relentlessly towards its goal. It keeps going until it finds it. Block its path, and it will go over, under or around you.

Its instinct to win is indomitable. In Summer it prepares for the Winters' (i.e., analogous to downturns in supply, recessed economy, etc). In Winter, it focuses its goal on Summer (it is positive, it knows Winters don't last).

It will do, or die.

In comparison, you are encouraged to succeed in Self leadership for 14 days. In trying to achieve it you will soon discover what determination you have for your Wholistic Success goal.

The world's greatest male dancer; Rudolph Nureyev, grew up in desperate poverty in Russia. As a boy he dreamed of becoming a great dancer but his father, a political commissar in the Soviet Army, would try to beat this out of him.

His storyline for Rudolph was the life of an engineer or doctor. Rudolph Nureyev faced his moment of truth at every beating and conquered not only himself, but the world of Ballet; a world requiring utmost Self leadership.

Get High on Results

We get paid for the results we achieve, not for the time we put into our work. The better the results, the bigger the reward.

If you are a sales manager and you require your sales people to make 12 calls per week, what will you expect from them at the end of the week?

Will you want excuses? Will you accept 8 calls per week? Won't you expect that at the very least the minimum number of calls are made even if no sales are achieved?

If you expect results of your staff, what results do you expect of yourself? Reverse the role for a moment. What if you had to report to your staff about the results you had achieved?

In business the result that matters is cash receipts. We need to set goals and procedures that give us the cash receipts to remain viable.

Developing your instinct to win-win in business is as easy as developing a passion for cash receipts. It doesn't matter how good your point of sale material is, how splendid your presentation, or how beautiful your letter-writing. Cash receipts are the arbiters of business success. Without them you have no cash-flow and all you are doing is financing your staff's livelihood through a burgeoning overdraft. Eventually, you will be the one to pay it back.

But results need time. How long would you give a child to learn to walk? On the other hand, how many years should your children stay in grade 5?

We need to aim for reasonable results in reasonable time while checking we are heading in the right direction and avoiding mistakes.

Develop an instinct for checking the major result areas each week. Whatever you find will give you a chance to smile, or to frown. Either way, you've got to know.

Play to Win-Win

Instincts for winning can be developed by playing to win.

Whether it's a game of cards, tennis, golf, a meeting at work or a sales call, develop the habit of taking it seriously enough to go for a win. You might not take home the prize, but you won by trying and therefore by reinforcing your success patterns.

In your work you win whenever you list tasks in priority order and do them one at a time. You win anytime you can say you completed a job to the best of your ability.

You win whenever you do willingly those things you don't like to do. You win when you produce quality work; give encouragement or display a Positive Mental Attitude.

You win when you go home knowing you got from the day, not through it; when you played to win-win, and everyone involved won in some way.

10

How to Negotiate to Win-Win

Whether you want a discount, a job, a meeting; to choose a restaurant; a car or a house or to gain agreement on a deal or to cancel it, the process is one of negotiation.

I am not talking about tricks, manipulating others or of the 'win at all costs' brand of negotiation. Negotiation is not confrontation. It should be a process of meeting needs and wants in a manner satisfactory to everyone.

Psychologist, author and speaker Dr Dennis Waitley says;

"Bullies make poor negotiators. That applies to verbal bullies as well as physical ones. Contrary to popular belief, negotiation is not won by intimidation. That only makes the other person defensive and resentful.

"The rules to successful negotiation are based on the principles of communication and co-operation. First, you want the other person to talk to you and, second, you want him to work with you. In other words, negotiation is the gentle art of persuading the other fellow that you can help him achieve his goals if he helps you achieve yours."

(From 'Personal Success Magazine')

In negotiation all parties bring their own perspective, needs, wants, deadlines, instructions, prejudices, limitations, etc.

A successful negotiation is one where all parties are satisfied. The outcome might not be the one they had sought, but one which they can accept with honour.

Major errors in negotiation occur:

- when you fail to consider the ability of the other party to negotiate

- when you don't consider what is acceptable to the other side

- when you escalate the problem or your commitment to it

- when you are overconfident about the outcome

- when you view success as 'win all or nothing'

To be a successful negotiator you need to consider the other party's position and have alternatives which could be acceptable to both of you. Also, it will be wise to include 'demands' which you are willing to remove by way of compromise.

These must be worked out before negotiations begin, then remain flexible enough so you can modify them in light of additional information gained during the negotiation itself.

For example, when Jan C Scruggs was planning his negotiation strategy to build Washington's Vietnam War Memorial, he decided to ask for two acres of prime real estate. He didn't need two acres. He asked for more than he wanted so he would have a point on which to compromise. The result? No one questioned the demand, so the memorial was built on two beautiful acres of rolling lawn in front of the Lincoln Memorial.

Negotiation begins when you listen; when you listen empathically; when you listen with a view to understand, not to reply.

Both parties must focus on beating the challenge, not on beating each other. To achieve this outcome and avoid emotional reaction we need to understand the elements of negotiation technique.

Information

The more you know about the other party's needs, wants, deadline, strength, etc., the more you will be able to influence the proceedings towards an outcome acceptable to you.

It is often to your advantage to know more about what they need and want than for them to know what you need and want. Yet few people take time to get as much information as possible about the other party before negotiation begins.

I am talking about research.

One way to do this is to send in a proxy; someone who has no power to make decisions but who can start negotiations. This gets you more information, can encourage the other party to show their hand or tell you where they stand. You can get involved later armed with vital intelligence and unfettered by any prior involvement.

At the meeting, get as much additional information as you can before you begin to negotiate. You can do this by asking 'open' questions.

Consider a simple case of everyday negotiation; the case of Peter M., a recently appointed salesperson with a large insurance company. Peter arranged an interview with Tom and Margaret B., a young couple who, unknown to Peter, planned to save for a deposit on an apartment within the next two years. They were both in well-paid jobs and already had most of the deposit.

Purchasing an apartment was their priority in life.

Peter M: *"There's a great deal of interest in pension plans these days. My company has the best in the market, earning (%) interest".*

Tom B: *"I think we're OK for now. Actually we're more interested in savings and ....."*

Peter M: *"There are no better savings than pension plans. They give healthy tax deductions, and you can retire in comfort ....."*

Marg B: *"Tom and I have thought about providing for a retirement income. But at the moment ....."*

Peter M: *"I know what you mean. There's always another bill to pay. But let me show you the cost of postponing your decision for just one year"*

Do you see the problem? Peter is trying to negotiate without information. This approach will soon turn into a frustrating experience for both parties. The following approach could be more productive.

Peter M: *"What is your main financial goal?"*

Marg B: *"To be rich"* she jokes.

Peter M: *"I can relate to that. But if you had enough money now, what would you do with it?"*

Tom B: *"I'm tempted to say; go off on a great vacation. But we're wanting to buy an apartment, actually."*

Peter M: *"When have you planned to buy, Tom?"*

Tom B: *"With a bit of luck, we'll be able to put a deposit down by the end of next year."*

Peter M: *"I can see that buying an apartment is very important to you. My company has a tax-advantaged savings plan that could really help. May I show you how it works .....?"*

In this case, Peter obtained information about the couple's wants and their deadline. With this knowledge he was able to negotiate a sale which satisfied the needs of all concerned.

Without knowing the needs and wants of the other party any negotiation will reduce to flogging a product, service or idea which might be totally unsuitable.

The result? No deal!

To obtain information, questions are the answer. These can be classified broadly into two types; fact and feeling questions.

Fact questions are for details such as age, size of company, location, quantity, date required, etc. Feeling questions provide information about philosophy, wishes, aims, wants, dreams, and so on.

For example, if you were negotiating to provide an office cleaning service, in your research phase you could ask;

Fact Question: *"Who provides the service for you now?"*

Feeling Question: *"Are you happy with their standard?"*

The fact question is important because it can tell you with whom you are competing. The feeling question can give you vital information about the other party's level of satisfaction.

Once you have this information you can propose your own deal. Negotiation can begin in the knowledge that you are on the right track. A win-win situation becomes possible.

The same applies when you are negotiating to win co-operation. First get information on what 'they' want, how they feel, their present constraints - in short, as much information as you can get. Lead with questions.

Simply knowing how another party works can be a great advantage. For example, let's assume you wanted to buy a new car. Knowing that most dealers work on monthly targets can help you get a better deal!

By postponing your negotiation until the last day of the month, dealers will be more likely to be flexible because they need to make target and put another 'dot' on the sales board.

Likewise with the purchase of an 'average' used car. In this case you can use the information that many dealers allow approximately $1000 to bring any trade-in 'up to scratch', another $1000 to defray costs of floor space and a further $1000 for profit.

Therefore, it is a reasonable guess that on an average used-car a dealer will try to sell a trade-in at $3000 above his purchase price.

Armed with this information of approximate profit margins and the sales manager's end-of-month pressure, you should be able to negotiate a better deal if your timing is right.

The car business uses the Japanese and Russian systems of negotiation: they send in proxies with no power to make decisions, then try to wear you down.

You, the 'prospect', deal with the salesperson. The salesperson has no power to make decisions. His job is to obtain a commitment from you, no matter how unrealistic, under which you will agree to buy *today*. He will then refer your proposal to his manager, who might accept it. Usually, his manager will send him back with a counter offer.

The sales person wants to go to his sales manager with a definite proposal like; *"I've got Tom S. who says that if we give him $XYZ on his trade-in he will pay $ABC for our car, right now, by cheque drawn on X Bank"*.

If the sales person does not go to his sales manager with an offer as specific as that, he is likely to be reprimanded and sent back for another try.

In this case the sales person is a go-between. He has to relay to his boss whatever you say. This system of preventing direct negotiation maintains the boss's image of authority and allows the salesperson to cultivate the impression that he is on your side.

The object is that if they can get you to agree to buy today, regardless of the practicality of your demands, they can work on you to be more reasonable.

Applied information is power. The more you have, the more you can influence a win-win situation.

Time

Former U.S. president Jimmy Carter brokered the Camp David Accord which brought peace between Egypt and Israel. The consensus of opinion was that he wore the protagonists down simply by using time; locking them into a process without an agenda so they each felt that as so much time had been invested, they'd better do something!

As a general rule the party who has an urgent deadline to meet usually makes the most compromises as the deadline draws nearer.

This knowledge is often shamefully exploited by negotiators at the highest level. By waiting until the eleventh hour they force compromise, often to that party's detriment. It is also exploited in everyday life. Here's an example:

Maria had five children. Her husband had preceded her on immigration to Australia the year before and now she and her children were to join him. To fund the voyage the family had to sell everything they owned, which included two houses, a blacksmiths' shop and a small farm - all at post-war ravaged prices.

She would need a considerable surplus to take to her new country because the rules were that immigrants couldn't bring towels, bed linen, crockery etc., and therefore many necessities would have to be bought on arrival.

The agent negotiating the sale knew that Maria had a deadline - her date of embarkation. Under instructions from the buyer the agent stalled, delayed, thought up excuses - anything to stretch out the payment of the balance of purchase moneys.

One week before her departure the agent informed Maria that the buyer had reduced his offer by 20%. Maria knew it was too late to find another buyer. It was also too late to take any legal action. She had a deadline. She had no choice but to accept the offer and borrow the balance from relatives to fund the family's voyage. The family arrived in their new country not only penniless, but in debt.

(I know this story is true because Maria is my mother. We emigrated when I was ten years old.)

That type of negotiation is the 'Win at all costs' brand. It goes hand in hand with the belief that if you can disadvantage the other party, you win.

There is nothing wrong with using knowledge of a deadline to your advantage provided it leads to a win-win result. Remember your core values; your Totem of Personal Excellence.

In his book; 'You Can Negotiate Anything', master negotiator Herb Cohen describes an incident early in his career when he was sent to Japan to negotiate an important deal. The Japanese negotiators wined and dined him, entertained him and even enrolled him in a crash course in Japanese culture. They did everything except begin negotiations insisting there was plenty of time.

Knowing that Mr Cohen had a deadline (a return ticket is a good clue) the Japanese negotiators skilfully delayed discussions until it was so close to the time of departure that Mr Cohen had to make concessions to return with a deal.

In his own words, his boss called it the greatest Japanese victory since Pearl Harbour.

Of the Japanese negotiating style, Donald J Trump says;

"I have great respect for what the Japanese have done with their economy, but for my money they are often very difficult to do business with.

"For starters, they come in to see you in groups of six or eight or even twelve, and so you've got to convince all of them to make any given deal. You may succeed with one or two or three, but it's far harder to convince all twelve."

If you're outnumbered, make sure you're not outsmarted. Plan your strategy and build in alternatives on which you can fall back.

Power

All too often 'power' is perceived, rather than substantive. Nevertheless our perception determines the approach, tone and conduct of negotiation.

For example, when you are negotiating for a new job, your approach to the interview and willingness to compromise would differ if you were the job giver and not the job seeker. That's because the job giver has the power to 'reward or hurt'.

In the main we tend to imagine the other party has more power and authority than it really has. Yet when we push, how often do we find ourselves confronted by a paper tiger? Is it any wonder that audacity so often wins the day?

A basic point to remember is to ensure you negotiate with the decision-maker wherever possible. It is not uncommon to negotiate for hours only to discover that the other party has to refer to a higher authority. This has been many a sales person's downfall.

Negotiating with intermediaries is quite common, especially at national level. The idea is that; *"Oh well, we can't really decide anything anyway, so you'd better make your offer as attractive as possible for our bosses to consider."*

There's no risk of an impulsive decision there.

Some negotiations are too complex to be settled in one meeting. Consequently it is vital to obtain as much information as possible (even about the decision-makers if you can) and to document the results of all meetings.

Following are some different aspects of power in negotiation:

Precedent

Car sales people often meet customers who tell them that 'Better Motors' down the road offered them the same car at a lower price and an additional $XYZ on their trade!

These customers are attempting to use precedent as a power factor. That is to say, *"Better Motors have done it, why can't you?"*

You too can use precedent as a power factor in negotiation. Consider the following conversation:

You: *"Your Company is well recognised as a supporter of junior sports. **Your donations to the junior league over the past five years have been of tremendous importance.** " (Precedent)*

They: *"Thank you. Our firm prides itself in being a responsible community neighbour."*

You: *"It's refreshing to deal with a company which has a social conscience. You might not have considered supporting the "Youth for ....." movement. However I believe its aims fit in well with your community neighbour policy."*

And another example:

You: *"I don't know if I can arrange for one hundred to be delivered by next Thursday. What if I can get 50 by Thursday and another fifty by the following Wednesday?"*

Them: *"That's no good. Wednesday's too late."*

You: *"If I could ask my Company to pull out all stops, deliver 50 by Thursday and the balance on the following Monday **just as we did with that order two months back**, could we go ahead with this order?"*

In a successful negotiation, no one loses. Each person must feel satisfied or it will come back to haunt you.

Patience

Have you ever been subjected to a sales presentation or negotiation that dragged for hours? Many use this 'patience' technique to obtain a commitment favourable to them. It works because you have made a large investment in time and therefore are keen to wind up the process, or you buy to get rid of the sales person or problem.

The more time people invest in a negotiation the more interested they become in concluding it quickly. Anyone who has experienced the Japanese style of negotiation will recognise the patience they display (i.e. getting you to invest as much time as possible).

"This is All I Have"

The power of a last offer has clinched many deals. However it is best to leave this as a last resort.

You: *"I appreciate that your XYZ is worth more, but I only have $XXX.*

Them: *"We couldn't accept that."*

You: *"I would pay more if I could but I don't have it. Would you at least consider my offer? Could you at least ask the boss?"*

Them: *"I'll check, but you're wasting your time."*

Does this approach really work? Let's see.

Two years ago I saw a beautiful painting for sale. The original price was $4,500 but it had been reduced to $2,500.

Me: *"I'd love to own it. But my credit card can only carry another $2,000.*

Gallery Owner: *"It's already been reduced by $2,000. I can't do better than that."*

Me: *"I appreciate that. It's so beautiful and worth more than I can pay. But $2,000 is all I have."*

Gallery Owner: *"In that case I don't know that I can help you. The artist ......"*

Me: *"Won't you ask him anyway. I'd pay more if I could. I know it's worth more ...."*

The gallery owner telephoned the artist who, tempted with the offer to sell then rather than risk waiting several more months, approved the sale. Worth a try, wasn't it? I saved $500.

It can work because the demand first trumpeted by the other party might not be their bottom price.

Winning in Round Two

Imagine an advertising agency carolling the virtues of their new campaign; Account Executives delivering a presentation full of commitment, enthusiasm and hype.

Them: (Wide eyed and brimming with expectation) *"Well? What do you think?"*

You: *"Sorry. But I didn't quite get it. Could you explain it again please?"*

Them:(Dismayed) *"Which part?"*

You: *"The whole thing!"*

Can you guess the effect? Who could go through a lengthy proposal a second time to the same audience with the same enthusiasm and commitment?

The same technique can be used in negotiation. Ask the other party to explain their proposal again. You might find their demands a little less firm and their willingness to compromise, enhanced.

Rapport

Establishing rapport and identifying empathically with the needs of the other party can provide you with the power of 'kindred spirits'.

That is to say, being helpful, genuinely interested in the other party's problems and needs and 'being on their side' will encourage the other party to compromise.

Whatever proposal or counter proposal you put, always point out how your offer or suggestion will satisfy their needs and wants.

Keep on Keeping on

Most people quit negotiating too easily. Persistence and determination are essential. Whilst often there are deadlines to consider, determination to 'see it through' can signal the other party that you must be taken seriously. This itself can give you power; the power of *purpose*.

In the end winning could rest largely on the technique you use. For example, if you can't get agreement on a major issue get agreement on the minor issues first (it might be easier for you to compromise on those). Return to the major issue later. They will have invested more time and energy which encourages a willingness to resolve the problem.

Summary

Learning and developing the art of negotiation can be a life's work in itself.

Skilled negotiators are sent abroad to deal with issues ranging from trade to diplomatic bungles to avoiding war.

Acquiring and developing negotiation skills is essential because so much depends on our ability to persuade, to put our case, minimise losses, enhance gains, obtain support, get a good deal and avoid being disadvantaged.

Getting a first 'No' is the signal for negotiation to begin, not to quit. 'No' means 'Not Yet'.

Effective negotiation is not necessarily a process of logic. You can have all the logic of an Immanuel Kant yet fail to persuade anyone because your logic does not provide what the other party wants. What they want can be related more often to feelings, ego and emotion, than to logic.

Neither is negotiation a battle to be fought. It is a process of discovery; of finding that point where conflicting positions can meet and agreement reached. So if you are ever faced with a negotiation involving a person you dislike, separate the person from the problem and focus on beating the problem, not the person.

Remember to take cultural differences into account. What seems 'The right thing to do' for you might not be so for them. Insults and cultural bad manners will only put the other party off side and hinder the chances of a satisfactory outcome.

Finally, always try to put yourself in the other party's place. If you were they, how would you like to be approached? What offers would you find acceptable or at least worthy of compromise?

If there are two golden rules in negotiation, they are these:

To get what you want, always offer something in return.

Sometimes it is wiser to say "No", and walk away.

11

How to Speak in Public

Public speaking is an effective method of furthering your standing in the community, your business or career. Through it you can:

- promote your business or profession

- sell confidence in yourself

- make valuable contacts

- earn additional income

It can also be a lot of fun and the mark of an accomplished self leader. Yet many people shudder at the very idea of speaking in public. They fear it. They don't understand that the audience is not against them; that the audience wants to enjoy the talk, not watch them squirm.

A talk is not a performance on which you are tested. So why be afraid?

As in most things, knowledge and correct preparation dispel fear. There are few (if any) 'natural born speakers'. There are those who can talk to groups all day long, but they are talkers not necessarily effective communicators or persuaders.

It is possible that you could give a straight-from-the-heart talk which would be enjoyed by many. However the issue is about effective communication. Without knowing, practicing and applying the 'rules' the chances of delivering an effective talk are greatly diminished.

No self leader would want to be as one of those who whimper, blush and cower from talking in public, because the ability to talk is a vital part of the ability to lead.

Here are the fundamentals of effective - and enjoyable - public speaking:

Analyse Your Audience

Who are they? Are they business people? A group of elderly lawn-bowlers, teenagers, musicians? Salespeople?

If you don't know, find out. Talk to the convenors and ask them for:

- details of the make up of the group, including age-range.

- what are their interests? What would they want to know?

- are there any current issues (humourous or otherwise) to which you can refer?

- who are the key people in the audience? (Get their names and titles right)

Determine Your Aim

is it to:

- entertain?

- gain support?

- call to action?

- inform?

- promote your business?

If the group's objective in having you does not fit in with your aim, you might want to consider whether you should accept the invitation at all.

Prepare Your Material

We tend to remember the details said at the beginning and at the end of the talk. It is a good idea to prepare interesting material to lift the middle. However add key points at the beginning (introduction) and at the end (summary).

Research your topic. Find interesting things about it. Get to know it well.

Prepare an outline of your talk in logical sequence. The following guide will help:

At the Introduction

include:

- a warm, empathic opening statement with a strong message

- what's in it for the audience? (What benefits will they get from listening to you?)

- what the talk will cover, what you hope to achieve

- when you will take questions (at the end of your talk, or throughout?)

- historical information of the topic (key points. Be brief)

- a vision of the future

In the Body of Your Talk

include:

- Outline of key points: (1 to 7), then support each point with information. For example:

  Key Point 1

  Support information A

  Support information B

  Support information C

Section summary statement

Repeat this formula for each key point or major section.

(Note: Try to limit your talk to no more than seven key points or ideas. Research shows the mind cannot retain more than these at 'one sitting' in short memory.)

In the Conclusion

include a:

- brief recap of the main points of your introduction

- brief summary of the 7 key points or ideas

- concluding statement

- call to action, exhortation, etc.

Check What You Have Prepared

- Does the material address the topic?

- Is it relevant to the interests of the audience?

- Does it flow logically?

- Does it meet your aim?

Determine the Need for Visuals

Research shows we absorb 10% of information through the ears, 20% through the eyes and 64% through the eyes and ears simultaneously.

Colourful, well prepared visuals can help us learn more and enliven a talk - provided they are not overdone.

Visuals include:

- overhead projection transparencies

- slides

- video tape/film

- flip charts

- whiteboard

- products or models

The most common visual means used are the overhead projector and whiteboard. Whichever you use will depend on the situation and aim of your talk.

Overhead Projector

- Keep one idea to one transparency if you can, otherwise mask your transparency to reveal one idea at a time.

- Use colour where possible

- Be brief

- Use diagrams or graphics where possible

Use of the Projector

- switch it off when you change transparencies

- use a pointer on the transparency *not on the screen* (i.e. face the audience, don't turn your back to them)

- use masks (a sheet of paper will do) to reveal complex information point by point

Video/Film

Don't let those take over your talk. Use them only to illustrate specific sections (especially where movement is required).

A clever, attention-getting short film can be a great ice-breaker at the start of the talk. An emotive film can be used in the same way to focus attention on a theme.

Visual aids are there to support, not replace the talk.

Choose a Presentation Strategy

Is the aim to entertain? Perhaps to inform in an entertaining way?

Use your creativity. Tailor your whole approach (serious, flippant, etc.) to your audience.

Think of 'attention grabbers' to focus attention. For example, if your talk is about 'violence in society' why not arrange an 'incident' and let the audience think it is really happening?

You could then walk onto the platform and begin your talk using the 'incident' as your starting point.

If you are talking to music buffs, an amusing story such as the one where Louis XVI of France asked his composer to invent an unusual instrument for the amusement of the court, could also amuse your audience. (The composer brought seven pigs which could squeal in a different octave. By pricking each pig in sequence he was able to play a tune.)

I used these principles to great effect when a lecturer at the Air Force's Officers Training School. One example: to demonstrate a charge and summary hearing procedure, I arranged 'an incident' where a corporal would be insubordinate to me in front of a group of newly-appointed officers. As far as the appointees were concerned, the 'incident' was genuine.

Everyone was uneasy as they witnessed the corporal's remarks, my answers and my order to a sergeant to place the corporal under arrest. Once the 'theatrics' were over and the murmurs in the group settled, I explained the whole situation and we proceeded to show the steps of preparing charges, arraignment, summary hearing and punishment.

By using imagination in this way, everyone became involved and enjoyed our presentations of Air Force law much more than they could have if we had lectured them.

Whatever you do will be influenced by how you decide to handle the presentation; by the tone you want to establish.

A word of caution here; be careful not to offend through risque humour or 'bad taste'.

Also, it's unlikely the audience will be completely ignorant of your topic. They want you to acknowledge that fact. So don't talk *'at'* or *'down'* to them.

Effective public speaking is 'talking the topic over with the audience'. You add sincerity, conviction, enthusiasm and a bit of yourself to bring the talk to life.

Address your audience as if you are speaking privately with each individual because they're listening to you for their own idiosyncratic reasons.

Prepare a Plan for Your Talk

It could take the form of key phrases on A4 paper or on palm cards.

The plan is for use during your talk and could contain:

- Notes to yourself (i.e. Smile, OHP, W/board, anecdotes, film, joke)

- Key sentences or words numbered sequentially

- Timing for each section

- Writing or typing should be bold enough so you can read it from a distance. Use highlighter pens to help separate sections of your talk.

Rehearse for Practice

By rehearsing you reduce your dependence on notes. This allows freedom to express yourself naturally and confidently.

By the time you are ready to deliver your talk you should only need a brief outline to keep you on 'track'.

Mark Twain quipped that it took him three weeks to prepare a good impromptu talk.

Rehearse for Delivery

This can only be done when you have rehearsed and know your material. Then you can concentrate on delivery. Here are some tips:

- Be 'conversational'. Don't preach.

- Deliver your talk in a 'friendly' way.

- Pause for effect. In other words, use silence to accentuate a main point. For example: *"To **achieve**. (pause ...) **That** is the alternative to despair"*.

  Well placed pauses punctuate a talk, add interest, and heighten our sense of expectation. They focus attention on the phrase following the pause.

  Actor Sir Ralph Richardson said; *"The most precious things in speech are pauses."*

Do's and Don'ts

Everyone appreciates:

- friendliness

- cheerfulness

- enthusiasm

- tasteful humour

- sincerity

- modesty

- good visuals

Few people like:

- being talked 'at'

- being talked down to

- sarcasm

- criticism

- unpreparedness

- ridicule

- arrogance

- preaching

When you 'rehearse for delivery', check you have not acquired any negatives. Build in positives.

How you approach and deliver your talk determines how well it is received (in some instances, to a greater extent than what you say!)

It is important to 'establish your credentials' as a speaker from the outset. Here are some guidelines:

Start with a warm, empathic opening, then strengthen it. You can do this by:

- **throwing down a challenge** (e.g. *"After today, none of you will be the same person you were yesterday; except by choice. If you have the courage, you can change your life."*)

- **using an anecdote.** For example (for a talk on fitness) *"A friend of mine has this exercise thing beat. Everytime he feels like exercising he lies down until the feeling goes away."*

- **asking an 'overhead' question.** For example (for a talk on financial security) *"How many of you could write a cheque for $10,000 right now - and not have it bounce?"*

A strong but empathic opening focuses the attention of your audience and gets them involved from the outset.

Explain what the audience will get (benefits) as a result of your talk. In other words, tell them why they should listen. For example:

Opening

"After today none of you will be the same person you were yesterday; except by choice. If you have the courage, you can change your life by applying what I'm going to reveal to you right now."

Why They Should Listen

"I'm going to share the secrets that made men such as Rockerfeller, Andrew Carnegie and many others enormously wealthy."

Tell them what you want them to do as a result of your talk:

"Take time to study the handouts. Apply the basics. Try. You've got to be here 'till you go so why not see how far your abilities will take you?"

Finish your talk with a strong, specific call to action. For example:

"The choice is yours. Success? or mediocrity? I urge you to choose success. I urge you to make the commitment. I urge you to reach out; to be first. Success is your destiny. Fulfil your destiny!"

Use the 'I' pronoun sparingly. Use 'we' or 'us' as much as possible. It conveys that you are one of the team.

Personal Points

Each of us has strengths in one area or another. For example, you might have a friendly, warm manner; a great voice, a certain 'presence'. You will want to emphasise your strengths and minimise your weaknesses (through practice). Here are some tips:

Voice

In public speaking there are few torments like a droning, monotonous voice. This 'quality' is an asset only to the hypnotist. However to the audience it is a frustrating ordeal.

When Albert Einstein was enduring such a speaker, he leaned over to his friend and whispered: *"I've just come up with a new theory of eternity!"*

Vary your tone of voice. Talk loudly, softly, pause, add enthusiasm. Your audience will love you for it and you will enjoy doing it!

Take care with your enunciation. Pronounce your word endings. This is especially important when using a microphone. (If you are using a microphone, speak a little more slowly to prevent your words 'blending'.)

Eye Contact

Effective speaking creates the impression you are talking to each person individually. Eye contact is essential for this. Look at people individually at all areas of the room. Preferably, maintain your gaze for a complete sentence.

Reading your talk prevents eye contact and, hence, we do not enjoy what in those circumstances would be a lecture.

Intensity, Commitment, Enthusiasm

Those are the elements which transform an ordinary talk into a dynamic oration.

You must be committed to your point of view. Be enthusiastic about the possibilities. Emphasise key phrases with conviction.

Anecdotes

Relevant stories which illustrate the point you are making breathe life into a talk and help your audience remember what you have said.

There are several books of quotations, humorous anecdotes, etc. which are readily available.

Humour

Your audience will be grateful for the judicious use of humour (if it is appropriate to the topic and relevant to the point being made). Be careful not to offend. Don't use sarcasm; racial, religious or sexist jokes, ridicule or risque humour. There always will be people in the audience who might be offended.

Use humour only if it helps illustrate a point or an irony. Leave unrelated jokes to comedians.

Rhetorical Questions

Asking a question and pausing to let the audience think can be a great device for involving everyone. Questions allow you to 'talk' with, not to them.

Positive Visualisation

Imagine your talk through. Imagine its resounding success. Imagine the applause of an appreciative audience.

Be Brief

If you can't say it in 30 minutes, consider writing a book about it instead.

Smile

A smile beams friendliness. Use it often.

Originality

Don't be afraid to use imagination. For example, if you are talking on 'enthusiasm' consider making your first few minutes as boring and unenthused as possible until you see the bored expression on the audience's face.

Then 'burst' with enthusiasm, making the point that enthusiasm makes all the difference, etc.

Use 'word pictures' to make a point. E.g. *"Don't just wade in, take a belly flop"*. Or, to explain the difference between involvement and commitment, *"It's like bacon and eggs. The chicken is involved, but the pig is committed."*

They make the point in an imaginative and 'visual' way.

Building Excitement

Varying the length of sentences is important. To build excitement use a string of short, sharp sentences. For example: *"Seize opportunity. Grab it with both hands. Strive to achieve. Reach out. Excel! Let nothing stop you!"*

Movement/Gestures

Don't be chained to a lectern. Move to the front of it, to one side of the platform or to the other. Movement creates excitement.

Use gestures sparingly and naturally. Don't 'force' them.

Nervousness

All speakers are nervous. Nervousness helps make achievement possible. It gives adrenain for best performance. Controlling nervousness is not difficult. Apart from slow, deep breaths before you begin your talk, the best control is thorough preparation and rehearsal. With everything prepared, what is there to be nervous about? *The audience is on your side.*

Final Points

Taking Questions

Tell your audience at the beginning of your talk whether you will take questions as you speak, or at the end.

There is no need to hurry your answer or buy time with "That's a good question" or "I'm glad you brought that up" etc. Simply pause, think and answer.

If you feel the question was not heard clearly by everyone, repeat it (especially as you have the microphone advantage).

If the questioner is emotional or angry, acknowledge his emotion before you answer. E.g. "I can understand why that would make you angry" etc.

Aim your initial gaze at the questioner, then as you proceed with your answer look at the audience generally so you do not exclude them.

Using the Microphone

Have your microphone positioned below your face, not in front of it.

Don't blow into it, tap it or say "Testing 1,2,3" etc. The equipment should be checked before you speak.

Speak a little more slowly and pronounce your word endings. Pronouncing the last syllable helps your audience distinguish between words.

Seating Arrangement

If the room allows, you can say how you prefer your audience seated. For example, a 'U' shape encourages audience interaction with each other. Theatre style discourages it.

Always check room layout, equipment and your notes before the audience arrives (get someone else to do it for you if you have no time).

Your Personal Introduction

Provide a brief 'resume' to the person who will be introducing you. This will save possible embarrassment for you, the introducer and the audience.

Handouts

Depending on the aim of your talk, well-prepared summaries can be a great idea. Tell your audience those will be available as they leave, etc.

Summary

We all engage in public speaking to some extent.

The social, career and business advantages you can enjoy by doing so effectively are well worth the effort and can enhance your reputation greatly. Nevertheless amidst your triumph, try to remember that 'thou art mortal' and maintain humility when you speak.

A woman once said to the great orator Sir Winston Churchill;

"Are you not thrilled to know, Mr Churchill, that everytime you make a speech, the hall is packed to overflowing?"

"Yes indeed," he replied. *"It is quite flattering. However when I feel this way, I always try to remember that if, instead of making a speech, I was being hanged, the crowd would be twice as big."*

12

How to Manage Time

We have already seen that hard work and good intentions alone are no guarantee of success. Effective work, which needs effective time management, can be one guarantee.

Rushing won't help. No one gets there faster than at the rate of 60 minutes an hour. The point is to manage the process so we get from time, not through it. To manage time well is money-making good.

We need to learn to deal with constant interruptions, doing too many things at once, not prioritising tasks, failing to delegate … to self-lead.

The late Brian Epstein is known as the man who made the Beatles. However he failed miserably when it came to delegating. Even as his stable of artists grew, he couldn't bring himself to delegate. The result was a frantically stressful life. In the end he died aged 32 of a self-administered accidental overdose of pills. His failure to delegate only pressurised his life. (There were other factors which led to his insecurity and unhappiness, despite his considerable wealth.) However had he been able to manage time he might have had the opportunity to live a more fulfilling life.

Managing time does not mean we have to organise every minute of the day. No one wants to work in a time straight-jacket. However to be effective we need to plan our day allowing for:

- a quiet hour to ourselves,

- time buffers to cater for the unexpected,

a prioritised list of tasks to be completed which might be:

- urgent,

- important,

- essential, or

- desirable but not essential

Whilst there are more complex systems for managing time, this section of the course deals with simpler systems which should serve you just as well.

The benefits should be evident immediately the systems are applied. You will have more, not less, time. You will be in control of your day, more relaxed and therefore less likely to make incorrect decisions. You will find time for long-term planning, recreation and concentration on achieving your specific Major Life Goal.

It is worth repeating that we are paid for the value we bring to the market place. The more effective we become the more valuable we are and the more wealth we will generate for ourselves and for others.

Following is a framework around which you could build your time management strategy:

How Much is Your Time Worth Per Hour?

Facing death, Queen Elizabeth I cried; *"A million of money for a moment of time!"*

Work out how much your time is worth by dividing the hours you work into the personal income you generate in an average week. Assuming it is $X per hour, use this to ask yourself: Is this filing, routine phone call, photocopying, etc., an $X per hour task? If not, delegate it to someone whose time costs less.

Limit Phone Time

Wherever possible limit each phone call to a maximum of five minutes. Learn and use polite ways to cut short a phone call, such as: "I'll need to go very shortly. Before I do what exactly can I do for you?"

This applies to incoming and outgoing calls alike. (A car phone can be an excellent time saver provided you are selective about giving out your number.)

Screen Phone Calls

If you have a secretary why not train her to ask:

May I *say* who is calling?

And what can I tell Mr .... that your call is about?

If it is a person you do not know you could train your secretary to say something like:

Mr ..... is unavailable at the moment, but if you care to leave your phone number I'll be sure to give him your message; or

Mr ..... can't come to the phone right now. He asked that you leave your phone number so he can return your call when he's free.

Can you see what these simple techniques are doing? They are giving control of your day back to you. The alternative is to relinquish this control to others; to follow rather than to lead.

Do Things in Batches

If calls, letters and memos aren't urgent why not schedule a time in your day and do them in batches? That way you won't be jumping from one thing to another then back again. Your thoughts won't be as fragmented and it will help reduce stress.

Simple Ideas Are Best

The humble manila folder can be a great help in organising your work, especially when you have loads of it. Try the following approach:

Divide your work into categories and raise a folder for each category. Place all the paperwork for each category in its respective folder. Prioritise and handle one folder at a time.

Raise a similar file for your key employees and superiors. You could call these 'Talk To' files. You will be able to place notes in them as matters arise without worrying that you'll forget to 'talk to so and so about .....'

Each morning review these files and schedule your calls or meetings in line with your daily plan.

On long drives why not use a recorder to dictate memos or give instructions? The important thing is to design a system for yourself, then use it.

Schedule Leisure Time

Fitness and health are important to good decision-making, productivity and key elements of your personal sphere of Life. If your work allows you the freedom, why not schedule some time for exercise or sport twice or more per week? Naturally, you'll make up for this time elsewhere. One hour per day should be feasible (even if you will have to lunch later?)

Write Everything Down

Much time is wasted because of poor communication or forgetfulness. General Charles Gordon ('Gordon of Khartoum') would bemoan even the loss of five minutes. He would sigh; *"Another five minutes gone! We shall never get it back again."*

Be a prolific note-taker. File your notes in appropriate categories. Accurate recall of previous discussions will keep you on track and save much exasperation and time.

Pay special attention to your letters and memos. If recipients don't understand clearly what you mean you will waste their time and yours unravelling unintended results.

Give little time to little things and big time to big things.

Learn to Say "No"

Do you believe that 'If you want a job done well you've got to do it yourself?' If so you could be in for a lot of frustration. The more you do the less effective you might become.

A common trap is taking on too much by not;

- saying "No", or

- not delegating

Saying "No" also applies for your superiors. You can do that by reminding them of other tasks and priorities you already have and that taking on a new task might prevent you from completing them. (If you are the only one who can do those tasks ask to reorganise your current priorities, thus expanding your time frame.)

Delegating is value for money. A good rule is; never do anything which can be done by a subordinate. That is good time and money management.

Be prepared to let others make their own mistakes but anticipate and check for them. If you teach them to do something well in the first place you can be confident about delegating similar tasks later.

Don't Become a Workaholic

Workaholics are more addicted to work than they are to results. Instead of being good leaders of self, they let work lead them. Over time they become less effective, stressed and can ruin their private life. Workaholics generally are not regarded as initiators and seldom become the Chief Executive. They centre their existence on the work/business sphere of life often to the neglect of the other spheres.

The addiction to take on more and more, work longer and longer hours etc., is unhealthy, as has been seen in the case of the late Brian Epstein.

Workaholics get by at first through sheer volume of work and some results. However time often shows their results are mediocre overall. Workaholics are much too busy chopping wood to sharpen the axe.

Set an Hour Aside for Yourself

Take a 'quiet hour' for yourself, perhaps first thing each day. This allows you to collect your thoughts and plan ahead.

Famous achievers who believed in the principle of a 'quiet hour' in the morning include Charles Dickens. He said; *"There is something incomparably solemn in the still solitude of the morning."*

Beethoven got up at daybreak, winter and summer, to start work. John Milton (author of Paradise Lost) got up at four in summer and five in winter. Goethe (German poet and legendary author of Faust) started work early. He said; *"I have never worked at night. I work mornings, where the gold lies."*

John Wesley, fiery preacher and founder of the Methodist Church, began work at four each morning; so did Alexander Von Humboldt (scientist and oceanographer). Antoine Lavoisier (father of modern chemistry) began work at six and continued until 10pm. Mozart started his day at six. The Famous German philosopher Immanuel Kant started work at five, so did Composer Brahms, and author Sir Walter Scott.

The list of early risers; of advocates of 'the quiet morning hour', is extensive.

In his book, 'The Techniques of Getting Things Done', Dr Donald A Laird describes how John Curran, a famous Irish orator and judge, made sure he got up at 4.30am each day. He explains;

"Exactly over my head I have suspended two tin pans, one above the other. When I go to bed, which is always at ten, I

pour a bottle of water into the upper pan, in the bottom of which is a hole of such a size as to let the water pass through it so as to overflow the lower pan at 4.30."

Julius Rosewald was one of the founders of the giant Sears Roebuck company. When he wanted to hire a lawyer he went to a lawyer's offices at dawn to see who came to work first. That was the man he hired and later took into the company.

Perhaps you could take your 'quiet hour' at home, incorporating exercise and breakfast?

Solve Problems Brought to You by Others - the Smart Way

Here's a time-saving technique for solving problems which are put to you by subordinates. Insist they put the problem in writing, clearly stating:

- What is the problem?

- What are the potential solutions?

- What suggestions do they have for solving it?

- Who is involved?

Many problems (especially minor ones) might never get to you because this technique allows a clearer perspective. Consequently solutions come to their mind and often they can deal with the problem themselves.

Make a 'Hit List' of Frequent Interruptions/Interrupters

Identify your most common interrupters and work out a way to minimise their impact on your time.

Does Your Boss Waste Your Time?

Are you often called to a meeting where your boss keeps taking phone calls while you just sit there?

Try slipping him a note saying; *"I can see you're busy. I'll come back when you have more time. Please call me when you're free."*

Place it on his desk upside down and leave quietly. (If you give it to him directly he'll read it and signal for you to sit back down.)

Be a Good Time Estimator

When you are given a job to do, estimate how long it will take and plan a time to do it.

Play 'Who's Got the Ball?' to Win

A favourite trick of subordinates and superiors is to keep passing 'the ball' to others.

For example, a subordinate may come to you with a problem and leave it to you to take the next step. (You've got the ball!)

Try to end each meeting with the next action being theirs (give the ball back). You'll be amazed at the time this can free for you.

Keep Deadlines Visible

Write them down and keep them in front of you until they are accomplished. This device will remind you and serve to focus your energies on the urgent tasks.

Without deadlines, tasks can be done anytime. As the old English proverb goes; *'What can be done at anytime is never done at all.'*

Meetings

If you are chairing a meeting start by expressing its purpose, how long it will take and your expectations of:

- what you want to achieve by its end,

- what contributions you want from delegates.

- Keep to the issues and don't allow side-conversations.

If you must attend a meeting ask to be there only when issues relevant to your area are being discussed.

Don't hold meetings up to accommodate latecomers. If possible, lock the door after the meeting starts. This encourages latecomers to be on time for future meetings.

Establish Clear Lines of Responsibility

Make sure your staff know what they should be doing, where their responsibility starts and stops and to whom they report.

When this basic rule of management is not applied it can waste an inordinate amount of time through misunderstanding, bad communication and confusion.

Handling Mail

If you have a secretary you could arrange for her to open all but private and confidential mail.

Have her divide mail into urgent and non-urgent batches and set aside 30 minutes to discuss it with her. Give your instructions directly (eg. file, distribute, bring forward in a month, etc).

Over a week this system can save you many hours.

Procrastination

The only way to start is to start!

Procrastination is a killer of time and procrastinators must like it better dead. Yet no one has the power to give us even one moment of time once we have used it all up.

If you must procrastinate, do it later.

Reward Yourself

Take a mini-holiday. Self leadership also means self-reward. Go to dinner! Buy a new shirt! We live and work for reward. So why not reward yourself when you complete a major task ahead of time?

The Daily Action Plan

The essence of managing time well is to:

- Plan your day; set daily goals.

- Organise your time to achieve those goals.

- Control your activity during the day to focus on those goals.

If you have a secretary, involve her in your plan (to help minimise interruptions, etc).

Accept that you are responsible for your day's outcome. It is up to you to lead yourself to get from, not through time.

The origin of the daily action plan probably came from American efficiency expert, Ivy Lee. At a meeting with Bethlehem Steel's Charles Schwab, Mr Lee proposed a service which would help the company manage more efficiently.

He suggested that after Mr Schwab had tried it, he could determine its value and send him a cheque for whatever he thought it was worth.

Within a few weeks, Charles Schwab sent Ivy Lee a cheque for $25,000 (at a time when $50 per week was big money!).

The system was:

- Write on a piece of paper the six most important tasks you have to do tomorrow

- Number them in order of importance

- Tackle item one until it is finished, then item two, etc. until they are all finished.

There it is! Simple enough, but it helped make Charles Schwab over 200 million dollars!

The daily action plan is not new. It's just effective. It's where time management starts. Sir Winston Churchill used it.

The following steps will help you design your daily action plan:

- Take a sheet of coloured paper and divide it into four columns.

- List your tasks in priority order.

- Do the essential things first.

- Avoid handling a job more than once.

- Delete each task from your list as you do it.

- Transfer any unfinished task onto the next day's list before you finish work.

Check the items on your 'desirable' column. If any have been there more than four weeks consider scrapping them (they might not need to be done at all, or at least can't be too important).

Be prepared to alter your plan as priorities could change during the day.

Such systems work very well. You might wish to alter them to suit you. That's fine. The vital thing is, whatever system you design; **use it.**

If you don't organise your day, it will disorganise you.

Your Diary

It is not wise to cram every minute of your day. Many things happen which are outside your control. Try to leave empty blocks of time in your day to allow for the unexpected.

These 'buffer zones' allow you to:

- enjoy more flexibility

- have more time to accomplish important tasks

The diary and daily action plan need to be used together if either is to serve you well.

Postscript

As for most systems, they will work well in controlling the ebb and flow of daily effort. However they can be less effective if your work is way behind or your section has a large backlog of things to do. The point is that to maximise effectiveness of any time management system, first you need to catch up. A system that has proven of enormous help to me is a variation of the Critical Path Forecast.

I used this when newly-appointed to a management role of an insurance company. The backlog of their accident and sickness division was daunting, with some tasks still outstanding after two years. Before I could think of organising the day to day workflow, I decided my priority was to clear the backlog so we could see more clearly.

I did this by:

- listing all outstanding tasks

- noting the job holder whose role it was to complete them

- asking each job holder to estimate the time it would take to clear his backlog

- determining which job-holder would need additional assistance to complete the work

- setting a specific date for all the backlog to be cleared

- listing all tasks in priority order

- drawing a Critical Path Forecast which listed each task, the day it was to be commenced, who was responsible for doing it, and the day it had to be completed. The action sheet consisted of vertical lines (one for each day of the month, noting weekends and public holidays. As I listed each task in priority order from left to right, I drew a dark horizontal line from the first day to the day that particular job had to be completed.

  (On the horizontal line I noted the name of those who had to complete that job. By the time the sheet was finished, it resembled a descending staircase of horizontal lines noted with the job to be done, the days in which it had to be done, and those who had to do it.)

- giving a copy of the sheet for the whole division, to each job holder, and having them tape it to the wall beside them so that as each job was completed, they could rule a line through it (that way, we could see progress being made)

- supervising each job and ensuring it was begun on time, and finished on time. By concentrating on this a job at a time, our backlog was totally cleared by the specified date, our agents were far happier because their new proposals and claims were attended to swiftly, our staff was much happier and I created an instant reputation within two months of joining the company. The result? I was promoted to a more senior position within six months.

Did the staff like my approach? Not in the least! They had a comfortable pace before I arrived, and they resented having to 'put in that extra effort'. In fairness I must say that had I been better at winning their co-operation, there would have been less resentment. However I had just resigned from the Air Force and my Air Force ways hadn't yet worn off. Nevertheless they soon got used to the freedom of being up to date with their work, and the division never slid back into chaos, even after I moved on.

It was only after the backlog had been cleared that I was able to put into place an orderly time management system. Before that, it would have been far less effective.

Summary

Twenty four hours, 1,440 minutes, 86,400 seconds; that's all we get each day; rich or poor.

What we do with our time, how well we use it and the choices we make ultimately determine success or failure.

Why not develop the habit of asking yourself; "Am I using my time effectively right now?"

Putting in long hours is not the important thing. What is important is what you achieve in them through Self leadership in time management.

13

How to Manage Your Money and Make it Grow

Do you know of people in their fifties who have worked hard all their lives but have not paid off their mortgage?

They might be hard workers, good workers, honest workers, but the best they can look to as a reward for a life of toil is the age pension.

They are Mr & Mrs Average; the majority of the population.

They cite any number of reasons for their plight. From them we can learn that hard work of itself, regardless how well it is done, is no guarantee of financial success.

As mentioned earlier in the course, in its 1992 list of Australia's 200 richest people, Business Review Weekly shows that only two percent inherited their wealth. The rest made it for themselves.

What factors make the difference between great wealth and poverty? Is one of those factors the ability to manage and grow money?

Consider Mr & Mrs Average who have worked for 35 years. Even at $20,000 per year for one and $10,000 per year for the other (adjusted for inflation and allowing the wife a break from full time work) they will have earned a fortune equivalent to $1.05 **million**.

Where did all this money go?? If they had saved and invested 10% they would have over $100,000! Add compound interest and they would have at least doubled this amount.

Ten per cent of their earnings could have made the difference between retiring broke and retiring with dignity, means and hope; retiring not *from* something but *to* something better.

Didn't they know they could have learned how to handle money successfully?

What happened to their plans? To their dreams? To their Self leadership? Were they sabotaged by financial time bombs?

Defusing Financial Time Bombs

One day soon the car you are driving will have to be replaced. Assuming this will be six years from now, how much will you need on top of your trade to buy a suitable replacement? $10,000? $15,000?

Where will the money come from? (Time Bomb No. 1)

If you are anything like Mr & Mrs Average you'll borrow the money and repay interest plus capital for a term of four to five years.

If you borrow $10,000, how much will you pay for your new car? Almost half its price again?

If so you'll be paying far more than the car is worth! By the time you repay this debt you might have to borrow again for another car and so create another 'time bomb'.

How Much Will Your House Cost?

Your mortgage of $100,000 over 30 years could mean repayments of over $250,000!! That's $150,000 of your hard-earned after-tax wealth you are giving away to someone else.

However a house is necessary, can be an appreciating asset and you save on paying dead money for rental, therefore it is a legitimate reason for which to borrow. But this does not mean you should be gifting $150,000 to your bank.

(Please note that you could take many years off mortgage repayments and save many thousands of dollars by electing to repay your loan fortnightly rather than monthly)

Other time bombs hidden in your house are the inevitable repairs, painting, etc. Where will you find the money?

Replacing Major Items

How long will your carpet last? Curtains? Refrigerator? Washing Machine? Television?, etc.

You know they will have to be replaced, but where will the money come from? (More Time Bombs)

Saving and Investing your money will teach you to make your wealth grow. Without learning this skill even if you have a windfall you might be unable to keep it.

Some people who win lotteries or those in 'The Lucky Sperm Club' who inherit wealth can soon lose it because they have never handled a substantial sum of their own money. They never learned the basic laws which govern money management. Here are two examples:

One*: Bill W. is a diesel mechanic who won a $1M Lottery. He bought a $0.5M house on a canal at Surfers Paradise, a BMW for himself, a new car each for his wife and two children and spent the rest on travel.*

The Result? When the bills came (canal fees, rates, etc) he couldn't pay. He had to sell up and move back to a less prestigious area. He lost thousands in legal fees and commissions, sold below market value and learned some of the fundamentals of how not to handle money.

Two: Under the headline: 'Lotto Winner Stole to Live' Brisbane's Courier Mail reported a story of a 44 year old man who had won $450,000 in the lottery and lost it on failed property deals. To survive he embarked on a stealing spree to *obtain money to live. Before his win, he was a successful Personnel Officer.*

It might comfort Mr & Mrs Average to say they did not know how money should be handled; that they didn't know about the need to secure an income stream. **But what stopped them from finding out?**

Their lifestyle was cratered by financial time bombs. Instead of paying themselves first, they paid others first. They were part of someone else's plans for their future. They were followers, not self-leaders. They lived a financial storyline written by others.

Through this chapter I hope I can spare you the pain of learning the hard way by showing you an easier way. But remember, whilst saving and investing money is easy to do, it is also easy not to do.

Firstly, let's look at the subject a little more broadly. This will help place the whole issue into perspective before we get into detail. Consider how financially astute people achieve financial security. They:

- Work out what they want (eg: to own their home, provide for their childrens' higher education, etc)

- List their wants in order of importance

- Start with what they can afford and add to it later

- Protect their family and income

- Stick to their plan.

They don't pay interest first and themselves last; nor do they put off making a start, no matter how humble that start might be.

Make a list of your 'personal beneficiaries'; the people you pay each week from your take-home wages.

(If you are like most, the grocery store is first on the list. Then there is the garage, the finance company, the bank, the credit card, the telephone authority, etc., etc.)

Have you completed your list?

Good.

Are *you* on top of the list?

What do you pay yourself? $__________

How much of your wage is yours to
keep and invest? $__________

If you are like most people, probably not as much as you would like. However what is more important is what you will do about it from now on, when you know the:

Fundamentals of Money Management

Following rules - even those as stimulating as for making money - will take Self leadership. It's always easier to enjoy an immediate gratification than to put it off for the sake of a future reward. Nevertheless managing anything well takes effort and in accumulating wealth there is an effort worth making. Here are the 'rules for ensuring your efforts bear fruit:

Rule One of Growing and Managing Money is:
Pay Yourself First and Invest It!

That should be 20% of your take home pay (but certainly no less than 10%).

By investing the money which is yours to keep, you make it grow in the following way:

- Capital (what you put in from your pay each week,) *plus*

- Interest, *plus*

- Interest on interest

Suddenly you have two workers to help you accumulate wealth. You will be amazed at how quickly your money will grow.

At 10% compound interest (that is, interest paid on interest paid on interest and so on) money doubles every seven years!

After a little time you will have accumulated enough wealth to convert it into an opportunity to make even more money (eg. buy a property,) In this way you will be adding a third worker to help your money grow: **capital appreciation.**

Without accumulated wealth, how can you take advantage of those and other opportunities?

Many people will say; *"But I need all the money I earn, to live. I don't earn enough now!"*

If you were unemployed you would have to survive on social security benefits! It would not be pleasant, but you would manage it. How? You would economise. You would spend more wisely. You would cut back on non-essentials.

When you have no other choice it is amazing what you can live without; even things which you now feel are essential.

For example, some people smoke away $20 or more each week. That's $1040 per year. Multiply this by 47 years (average working life) and by adding compound interest of 10% to this yearly amount they have set fire to a potential $998,579.00 to say nothing of damaging their health and polluting theirs and other people's air. (I am not trying to offend smokers. I am trying to point out where money goes and the opportunity costs associated with it.)

No one is asking you to cut back to the level of unemployment benefits; far from it. However if you want to accumulate wealth there is an effort to make; financial Self leadership. Don't spend first and try to save what's left, that's the method of the poor. Save and invest first, then spend what's left.

You can add yet another worker to make your money grow: **future pay increases**!

As you earn more through promotion or business growth, the amount of your regular 20% investment also increases.

Why do you need to be an effective manager of money?

Because one day you will have to stop working but the bills won't stop coming. That's the time you need money to work for you. That's the time people pay the price of following instead on self-leading.

Rule Two of Growing and Managing Money is:
If You Want to Build a House, Talk to a Builder

Many of us have well-meaning friends who seem wise and knowledgeable in all manner of things:- including money management. However if you wanted to repair a serious fault in your car, would you go to a carpenter or to a motor mechanic?

How wise is it to follow the investment advice of well-meaning friends if their job is not the daily investment of money?

By all means hear them out. Consider whether they have created considerable wealth for themselves through investment (including losses). But before you decide where, how and how much, would it not be wise also to talk to someone whose every day job is to invest money?

Additionally would it not be wise to spread your investments? Including investment in property?

Rule two of growing money is to seek investment advice from those who are qualified by training, knowledge and experience and whose job it is to invest money.

Rule Three of Growing and Managing Money is:
Manage Your Expenses

Don't confuse necessities with desirables. Before you spend, ask yourself; "How will this item help my money grow?" "What return will I get?"

Obviously many expenses go to maintain the lifestyle you want. Nevertheless with many of the major items it is possible to combine lifestyle with a dividend.

For example, you might want a fine house. Great! You deserve it! However be sure to choose a fine house which also has excellent prospects for substantial capital growth.

Another example; you want to decorate your house. Great. If you had the money, wouldn't you wish to choose paintings, vases, etc., which did the job you wanted (lifestyle) and also appreciated in value?

Not everyone is in a position to take advantage of those dual opportunities. However that is not a valid reason to neglect money management. On the contrary, managing your money is even more necessary.

Next time you purchase a substantial item (say, for $500 or more) ask yourself:

Will this article appreciate in value?

If I buy it, what is the opportunity cost? (i.e. if the $500 were invested at compound interest for x years, what additional income would it produce?)

Do I really need it?

You might buy it anyway. But at least ask yourself the questions so you know what you are doing.

How Do You Rate as a Money Manager to Date?

How much have you earned since you started
work? $__________

How much of it do you have left? $__________

What happened?

That simple exercise will have given you a quick glance at your money-management prowess to date. If you found it depressing, don't worry. Managing money is a skill which can be taught easily to willing students.

If you don't learn to handle smaller amounts successfully, how will you handle larger amounts? (Remember the diesel mechanic who won $1m - and squandered most of it?)

Rule Four of Growing and Managing Money is:
Protect Your Capital

If you want 'your ship to come in' you must first send a few ships out. Better still, climb aboard and steer them.

Your ships can be your capital. Whatever you do, make sure your capital comes back to you.

Here is an example: You want to invest $10,000 in XYZ venture for 12 months. Before you decide to invest you would satisfy yourself as much as possible that:

There was no risk to your Capital of $10,000 (by avoiding high return/high risk adventures).

The *worst* that could happen would be:

 You would recover your $10,000 because the investment was fully capital guaranteed, or you held a mortgage or security against it).

If inflation ran at 8%, you would earn at least $1200 interest because if you earned nothing, the value of your $10,000 would have been reduced by 8% (inflation) and it would be worth only $9,200 in buying power.

You could withdraw your capital whenever you chose or with minimum notice.

Obviously as your wealth grows so too will its earning power.

However it is futile to have the best plans for accumulating wealth if through some tragedy you were prevented from putting them into effect (for example, if you became totally and permanently disabled or left your family penniless in the event of your death) therefore:

Rule Five of Growing and Managing Money is:
Provide for the Unforeseen Time Bombs

A small amount invested each week will defuse those unforeseen time bombs. See an accredited Lifewriter from a major insurance company. Also, it is strongly recommended that you have a will prepared. Accepting our responsibility to others in this way is also a part of Personal Excellence.

Although life insurance and wills might sound depressing they are an expression of love for those who matter most in your life. Could you achieve wholistic success without them?

Rule Six of Growing and Managing Money is:
Borrow Only for Things That Generate an Income and/or Appreciate in Value

Wherever possible, borrow money only to purchase income-producing items. For example borrowing to buy a rental property might be preferable to buying a block of land.

The house produces rental income and capital appreciation, whilst the land takes up income (rates, taxes) and might produce capital appreciation over time.

(Of course the perfect block of land might do better than a less 'perfect' house. Nevertheless the principle of borrowing for income-producing items still holds true.)

Borrowing to buy an established business is another example.

Borrowing to buy a car (unless essential for your work) might not be such a good thing unless it is the type of car which appreciates in value.

It is not always possible to keep to this principle because our immediate needs often override the wisdom of saving and investing first. That is all the more reason to get to the stage where you don't have to borrow at all. You can do this by **paying yourself first** and investing it over time.

Become More Valuable

In 'Moments of Truth' I discussed the need for quality in all we do and 'putting in that extra effort'.

By keeping to those principles you will become more valuable. The more valuable you become, the more you will be paid (even if you have to change employers).

The more quickly you achieve that the sooner you will start to earn more. The more you earn, the more your personal pay of 20% which is yours to keep and invest, will be worth. By investing this greater amount you will earn more interest and more interest on interest, etc.

Be Prepared for Opportunities

It is an amazing thing that opportunities are attracted to those who have prepared for them.

Having a lump sum invested and watching it grow can give you a great warm feeling. The aim is to seek capital growth and a good return with minimum risk.

Don't be blind to opportunities (such as a good investment property). However exercise all the prudence we have already discussed.

Before making your decision, get the 'I've got to know' bug. Talk to those who are expert in handling investment properties. Talk to your accountant regarding the returns you would need. Study similar properties in the area and consider the average increase in value over the past 5 to 10 years.

Satisfy yourself that your capital (plus a factor for inflation and tax) is not at risk.

Patience and Time

Just as a tree needs time to grow, so does your 'tree of wealth'.

The magic of compounding interest needs time to work. Get-rich-quick schemes might work sometimes, but invariably are very risky.

Your aim could be to increase your wealth in the short term (say, five to ten years), which will give you an opportunity to accummulate wealth at a faster pace after that.

Be happy to succeed in smaller goals at first. Success in your Major Life Goal is the sum of your smaller successes.

Be reasonable with time and don't become discouraged. If you pay yourself first thereby ensuring that 20% of what you earn is yours to keep and invest, you can't fail to create wealth.

The remainder of this chapter deals with a basic money management system that can help ensure you defuse financial time bombs and obtain financial peace of mind.

If every family on limited income used a similar plan it would make an enormous difference to their financial situation. In any event it is strongly recommended that all serious students of Wholistic Success use this or a plan like it. By all means modify it to suit your personal situation. However start it now. Be a strong self-leader.

The Money Management System

Whenever the words 'Budget' or 'Money Management' appear, many people equate them with dieting or going without things they like.

Nothing could be further from the truth. The idea of managing money is to have more of what you like much sooner with the freedom that goes with it.

Here's how it works:

Step One

- Make a separate list of essential and desirable (but non-essential) items and their weekly cost.

- Total the costs for each group separately, then combine the totals ..

- Deduct the grand total from your weekly take-home pay.

Did you have a surplus? If yes, you can:

- Invest this surplus as money 'which is yours to keep and invest'.

If it is less than 20%:

- Look at your non-essential items of expenditure. Which can you do without to 'pay yourself first' at least 20%?

  (If you are serious about creating wealth you should feel no remorse in doing away with some non-essentials.)

  At the very least see if you can manage a surplus of 10% of your take-home pay NOW and increase this to 20% as soon as you can.

  (You are not losing non-essentials, you are gaining wealth which will grow!)

Step Two

If you are paid weekly, fortnightly or monthly you will have to calculate the yearly cost of each expenditure item and its proportionate cost, according to how you are paid.

For example, if you are paid fortnightly and your house rates are $1000 per year, you divide $1000 by 26 fortnights giving you the fortnightly expenditure for your rates of $39 (to the nearest dollar). (If you are paid weekly you would divide by 52, etc.)

Each pay you:

- pay yourself first and invest what is yours to keep and invest (20%)

- Allocate the rest of your pay to the categories of expenditure shown on your lists in the appropriate fortnightly, weekly or monthly proportions required.

For record keeping and ongoing money management you will need to follow the following guidelines:

1. Purchase a ledger (18 columns or more as needed).

2. Identify your:

   Usual categories of expenditure from your lists.
   Your future items of expenditure (time bombs).
   The amount of money you have in cash now.

Step Three

Enter one category heading for each column in your ledger.

Step Four

Calculate how much money you should already have in each category to meet expected bills. For example, if you are paid **monthly** and receive a rate notice for $600 in June, assuming it is now January, under the **house** category you should allocate $300 for this item now.

Similarly, if your house and contents insurance premiums are $400 per year and they are due in August, you should have four month's of the $400 ($133.33) in this category because you only have eight months to go before they are due and payable.

Step Five

Allocate the cash you have in the bank to those categories, to 'catch' up on your monthly allocation to date. If you have any 'surplus', allocate at least 20% of the surplus to the **'mine to keep and invest'** category and spread the balance over the remaining categories as you consider prudent (don't neglect to provide for a Replacement Fund (Financial Time Bombs).

Step Six

Each time you are paid, allocate your pay according to the need for each category by completing a book entry.

Step Seven

Each time you withdraw money, complete a book entry.

Notes

The last amount in each column must reflect the cash held for that category at any one time. Therefore equations are cumulative.

Audit your calculations regularly to pick up arithmetical errors. Check your **total** against your bank books.

Persist. If you do not have the Self leadership to manage small amounts, how can you be trusted to manage larger amounts? Once set up it will only take a few minutes each payday to update.

Don't despair if you discover you do not earn enough to pay yourself first and invest it. It gives you all the more reason to spend wisely and work to succeed as quickly as possible.

Whenever the combined funds in the 'Mine to Keep and Invest,' and 'Item Replacement Fund' categories exceed $500, you could transfer them to a capital guaranteed investment which provides access to your money, a good rate of interest and tax advantages.

Remember to add other 'surpluses' and interest accrued from other sources.

Whenever you get a pay increase, allocate a least 20% of the increase to the 'Mine to Keep and Invest' category first and spread the rest as you judge prudent.

By managing your money in that way it will not only grow surprisingly fast, but give you much satisfaction and financial peace of mind.

Enjoy it! You will no longer be alarmed by an account in the mail. Simply refer to the appropriate column in your ledger and you will see that the funds are already there.

Do you want to buy clothes? Take the worry out of agonising whether or not you can afford them. Refer to the appropriate column in your ledger and if there is sufficient money allocated, enjoy yourself!

Perhaps you would like to take someone to dinner? Again, refer to the appropriate column and bon appetit!

As time elapses and you need to replace a household item, furniture or car, refer to your 'Item Replacement' column and you will know what you can afford.

Summary

By using this system you will control your money. You will be in charge; no more nasty shocks.

But beware the trap! A column may show an excellent deposit 'just sitting there' - don't be tempted! It is there for a future expenditure (time bomb).

The car will need replacing, and by paying cash you **will save thousands of dollars in interest payments**. Don't pay for the present by robbing from your future.

If you do nothing else, keep this rule: *save 20 per cent of your take-home pay and invest it.*

It can keep you.

14

How to Design your Life Blueprint for Your Success

Would you board a ship if you knew the captain had no idea where he was going, had no navigational charts, had not checked to make sure there were enough fuel and provisions and did not realise the crew was about to mutiny?

Would you build a house without a plan?

Isn't the principle just as relevant to someone embarking on a life success journey without a blueprint for its achievement? Self leadership is all very well, but where are you going to lead yourself?

If you don't have a blueprint for your success you will be part of someone else's blueprint for theirs. Someone else might not plan very much for you. You will be living a storyline written by others with no guarantee of a happy ending.

The Chinese philosopher; Confucius, said: *"In all things success depends upon previous preparation, and without such preparation there is sure to be failure."*

Your blueprint for your success needs to be a storyline written by you; It needs to be your plan to live life by your own design, not by default.

It will be a blueprint for your business/work sphere of life, not just a series of statements and promises to be written then quickly ignored.

Your Blueprint should also be flexible enough to accommodate change as you and your needs change, enabling you to check progress regularly so you don't lose sight of who you are, where you are going and why you want to go there.

Before you start on this vital task, consider what the master strategist himself - Napoleon - had to say about planning: *"Men take only their needs into consideration - never their abilities."* You too will have many abilities to take into account.

Plan to do; to lead yourself to your destiny. It is pointless designing the best looking blueprint for success if it comprises a catalogue of promises which you don't intend to keep.

Someone once said that "Goals are dreams with a deadline". Make your goals big enough to excite you into action, but be realistic about their achievement and with time. Here's a refresher on the art of goal setting:

Goals - the Basics

- Start with your specific, Major Life Goal.

- Determine the spheres of your life in which you want success, and the extent of the success you want.

- Divide your Goals into long term (to retirement,) medium term (5 - 10 years) and short term (1 - 5 years).

- Face reality as it is, not as you wish it to be.

- Don't hurry. Make sure these are the things you really want. What *could* you be?

- Each goal should describe a specific result and set a date for its achievement.

- A goal should be ambitious yet achievable.

- Don't use vague terms such as "Wealthy by the time I'm in my forties"

- Almost everything we have learned has required us to: try, fall, adjust and try again. We learned to walk, talk, swim, drive, etc., in the same way. Prepare for and anticipate falls.

- Goals should need you to do more, or to do it better or differently.

- Your goals need to be flexible enough to change as your needs change. In ten years you might not want the things you want now.

- Reward yourself each time you achieve a goal (a dinner, new shirt, shoes, etc).

- Share your plans with someone you respect.

- Include family and personal time in your plan.

- List your reasons for wanting success.

- Question your motives for wanting each goal. Make them honourable, in keeping with your Totem of Personal Excellence.

To help you consider your personal blueprint I have listed a framework of topics which you might wish to adopt. Whether or not you choose to adopt them is not important. What is important is that you invest a few hours into the rest of your life, prepare a written plan on how you will live it and achieve Wholistic success through Self leadership and Personal Excellence.

Suggested Topics for Your Life Blueprint

The aim of your blueprint is to help you answer the following key questions:

Where Am I?

Consider where you are in view of the past five years. What progress have you made in your business/work? Are you where you wanted to be? Life will change for you only when you change. Consequently part of your answer needs to take your self-perception into account.

Where you are also needs to include your present financial and family security.

Once you have determined 'Where you are,' ask:

Where Do I Want to Be?

Divide your specific goals into long term, mid term (one to five years) and short term (your next twelve months, your next month, next week.) Your long term goal will be your specific Major Life Goal. In other words, what do you want to have achieved by retirement? Will you be retiring *to* something or *from* something?

To be effective, goals need to be specific and measurable. Next to each goal you will need a date for its achievement, what you will do to achieve it, any obstacles you might encounter and details of how you plan to overcome them.

To consider how you will achieve your business/work goals you need to answer the following questions:

What is my 'Best-Client' profile?

What are my specific markets?

What products will I provide to my specific markets?

What are my monthly cash needs including a surplus to fund my goals?

How am I going to get to where I want to be?

What training and support will I need?

Check your records for a 'profile' of the type of client who provides most of your business.

What is My 'Best-Client' Profile?

Age:

Occupation:

Single/two income family:

Children:

Income group:

Other:

Treat your 'best client profile' as a specific market. Other markets could be: Self-employed; Professional (eg. Managers, teachers, doctors, etc); Young Adults, etc Align your activity to specific markets, not products. The markets you choose will determine the product mix you will need and, hence, your income.

What Are My Specific Markets?

Best-Client Profile Market:

My 'Natural' Market:

Market 3:

Market 4:

Market 5:

Your next step is to determine the cash you need each month to meet the known expenses and surplus to fund your goals. Check progress each month to ensure you are on target (or, if not, how much you need to make up in the following month.)

Now you know where you are, where you want to be, your specific markets and monthly cash needs. The remainder of your blueprint helps you answer:

How Am I Going to Get to Where I Want to Be?

This is your business roadmap. It will guide you to your selected destination. Before you get down to specifics, determine your 'mission statement'. This is your business philosophy; the way you will carry out your work with Personal Excellence.

My Mission Statement is:

I encourage you not to bypass this step. A mission statement is a compass. It will guide you through many of the inevitable ups and downs of life.

When you have determined your mission statement it will be important to consider your strengths and weaknesses. Those can be bolstered by effective training and support, so an important question to consider is:

What Training and Support Will I Need?

This can be divided into:

Training needed and date to be completed

Support needed from your partner/spouse

Support needed from your office

Assistance you will need from your manager (eg. weekly talk)

When you have the answers to those questions it will be time to roll up your sleeves and get down to framing a specific programme that will achieve your goals. The following questions will help you do that.

What is My Specific Action Plan?

For example, include any special promotions or campaigns you could undertake to increase business and productivity; to cut down on absenteeism, etc. Also, consider:

Obstacles to overcome (eg. time management)

How you will overcome them

How you plan to monitor your progress

Your life blueprint could need to include ways to increase your income so you can fund your goals.   In that respect it would be useful to spend some time considering your marketing strategy to see how sales of your product or service can be increased.

Professional business people market concepts but sell products. Choose the concepts you feel most suitable for your specific markets and plan a promotional strategy for them.

When you have finished that task you will have completed your blueprint for your financial and work sphere of life. But what are your goals for the Family Sphere? Financial Sphere? Personal Sphere? Community Sphere? Spiritual Sphere?

Those might not require the detailed analysis you have just worked through. Nevertheless they are of paramount importance and I would recommend that you set specific goals for each of your life's spheres to ensure a well balanced and Wholistic blueprint for your success journey.

If your individual life blueprint involves the start or expansion of a business, the following guidelines for a business plan could be of help.

Format of a Business Plan

Your business plan will help you:

- determine if your idea or business venture is viable,

- itemise resources, determine funding, clarify concepts and detail a plan to achieve your goal,

- with 'signposts' so you can measure progress,

- present to bankers, investors, accountants, prospective partners or any party who might help or become involved in your venture.

Your plan would include the following sections:

The Cover Page

This should identify the concept/subject of the plan and the title and name of the plan's designer.

Contents

List the various sections of the plan. This helps the reader get to the information he wants, quickly. It also gives your plan a professional touch and shows you are really serious about its achievement.

Summary

State the nature of the venture and what it offers you (and to any prospective investor). Usually, the summary takes up to two pages, rarely more.

This tends to be the first page read by a prospective investor because it gives him a precis at a glance.

Product Profile

Outline: the nature of your product or service, explain its background. Who invented it? What research was carried out to determine a need in the market? Do you have firm offers to manufacture or distribute it? Do you have orders to fill? What competition will you be facing? What are the opportunities for expansion?)

Management and Organisation

Describe how you intend to organise and run your project. Who will manage it? What is his background? What staff will you need?

The Operation

This is the 'guts' of the plan. It includes forecast of cashflow. For example:

Sales income (projected)

Cost of product

Net income

Expenses

Current cash position

Forecast for first three years

Annexures

In the annexures are contained support information, documentary evidence, resume of managers and directors, details of any research undertaken, brochures etc.

No two business plans are alike and usually their purpose is to provide an overview of the business and projected profits.

The main thing to remember is that almost nothing ever goes strictly according to plan.   Therefore, it is wise to build in reserves and leeway, to be modest with your forecasts and give yourself more room than you think you might need.

Postscript

Preparing such a detailed analysis for achieving what you want in life might seem a lot of unnecessary trouble. After all, no one is going to walk around with all that detailed information inside his head.

The aim of working through the process of such a blueprint is not to focus on the nuts and bolts of it. It's like driving around in a fine automobile. You enjoy what it does and where it can take you. You don't need to visualize the crankshaft turning inside the block.

Once you have your blueprint written down you will benefit through:

- knowing what is your specific, Major Life Goal
- how you will realize it, and

- that you have a thorough plan for its achievement.

That comforting knowledge is all you will need to carry.   The plan itself can be divided into weekly or monthly steps, and if you plan to achieve each step at a time and do so, then all you need to worry about is your next step.

(If it would help and encourage you to complete your life blueprint you could send for a detailed format which includes specific areas for you to complete. All you would have to do is to fill it in. For information write to The College For Success Studies. PO Box 503, Springwood 4127, Australia enclosing a reply-paid, self-addressed envelope.)

The Wholistic objective is to achieve wealth, health and happiness through Self leadership and Personal Excellence in a way that enriches others and benefits your community.

Your blueprint for your success is more than a catalogue of goals; it is your own script for your future. It is the point where Self leadership - and your better tomorrows - begin.

15

Your Spiritual Dimension

After years of research in compiling this book I have concluded that no system of success embodying happiness can be complete without reference to human spirituality. There was simply no way I could ignore the fact that a great many successful people all over the world are also deeply spiritual. Bypassing that fact would have meant presenting only part of the wholistic success equation.

I am not going to try to convince you there is a 'God', a 'Force' a 'First Cause' or some other 'Supernatural Being'. No one can do that for you but you. The aim is to show, in a few brief pages, that people who are somehow linked to the spiritual side of their nature tend to be *happier* despite the level of achievement they might enjoy in their other spheres of life.

Consequently spirituality is discussed in the context of achieving happiness, not in the context of religion.

(Interestingly, the essential point of most religious figures, including Jesus, was to teach people how to achieve and live a happy and successful life based on mutual respect, caring, integrity and faith in the benign fatherhood of (God). The other interesting point is that if you, like me, were to undertake research of success experiences dating from 2,500bc to the modern era, you would find that all the central precepts for achieving personal success; wholistic success, are contained in the Bible!)

But the central question remains for each of us: *"Why bother with getting in touch with our spiritual dimension in the first place?"*

Well, for one thing, no one on his death bed has ever been reported as saying *"I only regret not having had time for more work."*

Spirituality means different things to different people. In his autobiography, the great Irish flautist James Galway relates how after an accident he lay close to death in hospital. He took the time to reflect on his life and decided that from then on he would give each performance as if it were his last. When people hear him play he wants them to have a feeling they are listening to 'the voice of God' through him. (James Galway - an Autobiography)

Teilhard Chardrin wrote; *"We are not human beings having a spiritual experience, we are spiritual beings having a human experience."*

John Ruskin said; *"Really great men have a curious feeling that greatness is not in them but through them."*

Psychologist Dr Susan Jeffers, in her book; 'Feel The Fear and Do it Anyway' says of spirituality:

"I believe that what all of us are really searching for is this divine essence within ourselves. When we are far from our Higher self, we feel what Roberto Assogioli has so aptly called 'Divine Homesickness'. When you are feeling this sense of being lost, or off course, the thing to do to find your way home again is simply to use the tools that will align you with your Higher Self - and thus to allow the good feelings to flow once again."

But what about hard headed businessmen? Here's one example.

At thirteen years of age John Fairfax left school to serve an apprenticeship with a printer so he could help with household expenses.

After a failed business venture in England he emigrated to Sydney, working as a journalist, librarian and at any other work he could find. However he was not the type to live a storyline written for him by circumstances.

In time he would own one of Australia's largest newspaper groups, help found the country's largest insurance company and become a trustee of the Savings Bank of New South Wales.

Throughout his life he kept in touch with his spiritual roots serving as Deacon of his church and as President of the YMCA. His belief served as the foundation for his life's work.

Known as a man of honour, John Fairfax returned to England to repay debts he had incurred many years before he had left his native Warwickshire.

There are, of course, countless other examples and you would know of many of them. However it is interesting to look at the view of noted Professor of Mathematics at the University of Adelaide and author of 20 books: Paul Davis. He observes that since Copernicus, man has been alienated; moved away from the 'centre':

He further states that the laws of physics make consciousness inevitable. He sees this in the growing complexity of the universe. For example; its beginning in void, then the appearance of matter, expansion, the appearance of chemistry, then Biology and ultimately; consciousness as the inevitable next step in the 'design'.

He concludes that this sequence; this ordered evolution, implies a deeper meaning underpinning the universe. (From an Interview on SBS Television, 22 Oct 91)

Whether you agree is not important. The issue is whether you can achieve a deeper happiness that will accompany you through life by keeping in touch with your spiritual dimension in whatever way you choose to define it.

A Psychiatrist who survived the horrors of three Nazi concentration camps: Dr Victor Frankl, gives an indication of spirituality when he writes;

*"The experiences of camp life show that a man does have a choice of action. There were enough examples, often of a heroic nature, which proved that apathy could be overcome, irritability suppressed. Man **can** preserve a vestige of spiritual freedom, of independence of mind, even in such terrible conditions of psychic and physical stress.*

"We who lived in concentration camps can remember the men who walked through the huts comforting others; giving away their last piece of bread. They may have been few in number, but they offer sufficient proof that everything can be taken away from a man except one thing; the last of the human freedoms to choose one's attitude in any given set of circumstances; to choose one's way.

"The way in which a man accepts his fate and all the suffering it entails, the way in which he takes up his cross, gives him ample opportunity - even in the most difficult circumstances - to add a deeper meaning to his life."

(From 'Man's Search For Meaning')

It is true, of course, that one can accumulate wealth and enjoy health without being spiritual. However how many of those who have done so can be said to be wholistically successful? Did they achieve happiness? Did they discover fulfilment in their life?

The former Soviet Union made itself a non-spiritual State by law. It forbade any form of spirituality and actively persecuted adherents for 75 years! Were the people happy? Did they become wealthy individually or as a nation? Quite the opposite is true.

Of course there were many other factors responsible for the misery and deprivation suffered by the Soviet people. Nevertheless the point is that by denying a people's spirituality no compensating benefit became apparent.

Whether or not you believe in an intelligent force which pervades and maintains life is a matter for you. It is not my intention to proselytise.

However it must be said that for many successful people spirituality seems to provide a solid foundation for their life; a sense of 'partnership' with a 'Life Force', a strong sense of value and purpose; of a higher self; of the quest for Personal Excellence.

Spiritual people seem to handle life's major crises with more courage and strength. They tend to be more resilient and in times of trouble find sources of power within themselves.

However the frenetic pace of modern life tends to distract us from seeking deeper truths. Howard Crago, Noted Australian Journalist, writes;

"Modern life is against looking out of the window or, as some would say, looking into life. It's pace constantly accelerates. Demands on our time continually increase. Much of this action aims to increase the possessions that satisfy our physical and emotional needs. Yet it can deprive us of the chance to grasp other, less tangible, but more satisfying and durable possessions.

"These include buried memories we can be too busy to recall; ideals and aspirations we do not stop to define; and an appreciation of 'the mysterious affinity binding together ..... religious truths, aesthetic beauty and moral goodness."

(From 'Spare a Minute')

And it might be this frenetic pace of life in the guise of 'modernity' that makes so many people look upon spirituality as 'old hat', as out of context or simply as irrelevant. After all, nowadays we journey into the heavens! So why risk embarrassment?

One of the joys of serious research is that the researcher often savours many delicious ironies of spiritual wisdom. For example, Australia's Aborigines are probably the oldest surviving race which didn't choose to develop a material culture beyond the level of the stone age. (They didn't have to. Instead of our modern approach of changing our environment to suit us, they changed themselves to suit their environment, and lived in perfect harmony with it.)

They chose instead to develop a complex theory of the universe and creation which they call the 'Dreamtime'. According to Anthropologist David Maybury-Lewis, their explanation of the creation is much closer to the theories of our most eminent theoretical physicists than are the beliefs held by most 'modern people'. (From an interview on SBS Television, 13 August 1992)

How does one explain an 'intuitive' wisdom that can bridge a 60,000 year chasm?

That life is 95% thought, 5% form you proved for yourself when you reached out to 'snatch a moment of life' earlier in the course. Given that truth, is it really any wonder that life itself should contain a spiritual dimension and, with it, an intuitive spiritual wisdom?

Whether you are a Christian, Moslem, Hindu, Buddhist, Jew or an adherent of some other religious system is not central to spirituality at all.

In the end we are all on a voyage of growth, learning and discovery. Our paths might diverge, but our destination is a common one.

Each system provides its own road map. The fool who interrupts his journey to claim he has a better road map than someone else is a fool indeed.

Personally, I have been a religious person as far back as I can remember. My earliest ambition was to become a priest. I even saved my pennies to prepare for that day. However I abandoned that idea by the age of ten.

I think the attraction for me was that the priest in Caraffa, the small village in Southern Italy where I was born, was a man of very strong influence. Everyone seemed to look up to him. He was so much at the centre of all the festivals and was invited to all the parties that I immediately thought: that's for me! I even wanted him for my Godfather.

I continued to have a deep interest in religious affairs until the age of 30. Up to that time I had been involved - off and on - with various churches. At times I took an active involvement.

However it wasn't until January 1977 that I changed from being a religious person into a *spiritual* one. Some would describe the event as a 'born again' experience. It was exactly that.

In one moment, I experienced a coming together of many insights. For the first time I understood a wider purpose and realized that religiosity, when dogmatic, is a great hinderance to a deeper - almost intuitive - understanding of our spiritual dimension.

I understood theological concepts far more clearly and in a more exciting way. Blinkers fell off. I no longer needed to believe. **I knew.**

Did I feel the urge to tell everyone about my 'born again' experience? Not on your life! It was mine. I wanted to keep it. I was so elated at this boon, this mysterious infusion of understanding that I couldn't sleep for days. The awesome thing was that I seemed to recognise its source!

From that time my life changed dramatically. I feel a sense of partnership with my spiritual self. I feel as if I am walking with a spiritual companion who guides me and helps me see that trials and setbacks are merely learning experiences; that life is mostly thought, not form.

I know how easy it is for anyone engrossed in their work/financial sphere of life, especially those who operate their own business, to block sensitivity for issues other than those pertaining to that sphere. This is not necessarily intentional. The nature of competition can force a major focus on business issues and distance other matters.

That is not to say that everyone should join a church, temple or mosque.

I can only speak for myself and as far as I am concerned I have been blessed with a precious gift which, despite what any cynic might say, I would rather have than all the money in the Bank of England.

Is my experience common? I don't really know.

What **is** common to spiritual people is that when they tap into their spirituality for strength, they get it!

To the practitioner of wholistic success spirituality is enjoying a personal relationship with the deeper meaning of creation. You don't need to go to a Church, Temple or Mosque to achieve that or to live a life of Personal Excellence.

The organised religions through which millions have been killed, tortured, or used as a pretext for war down the ages, were concerned more about money and power than about spirituality.

An individual's spirituality cannot be fought over or taken away from him. It is a personal relationship; an understanding between himself and a deeper meaning of life.

You can call this 'deeper meaning' 'God', 'Allah', 'Jehovah' or any other label you wish. That's your perogative. In any event it is not that important except as a reference point.

In his eighties, Dr C.G. JUNG was asked if as a young man he believed in God. He replied that he did. He was than asked; "And what about now, after a lifetime of exploring the human psyche?" Dr Jung replied; "Now I don't have to believe. I know!"

Helen Keller, the famous blind, deaf and mute girl who captured so many hearts with her courage and strength, when asked about God said: "I knew Him. But I didn't know His name".

They called this deeper meaning 'God'. However if you asked them to define 'God' you might not get a common definition at all.

A spiritual person knows. He does not merely believe. He knows his spiritual source and draws from it strength, peace, goodwill and sure footing for life's journey.

The decision to nurture your spiritual dimension could give your life deeper meaning; mission; fulfilment. It could also give you strength to deal effectively with the lows that are such an inevitable part of life.

I don't think I could express the benefits of getting in touch with your spiritual dimension more eloquently than this:

"I continue to prosper because I know what gives me purpose on this Earth."

How can it be a happy life; that life which is bereft of a deeper meaning?

Health, wealth, *and* happiness are your birthright. I encourage you not to settle for less.

16

A Final Word

Over the years I have spoken to many people on how they could enhance their level of success. When I met some of the same people years later, I often found them still at their former level; struggling to achieve that elusive pot of gold at the end of their rainbow.

Yet they frequently attend motivational seminars. Do courses. Talk motivation. Read books. Some of them dream of writing books on 'the meaning of life'; of counselling others; of being mentors and gurus; of achieving great deeds.

So why is it that 'success' eludes them?

A common factor is that many of those people are still struggling to achieve the most fundamental success of all; self acceptance. They want and strive for 'success' to prove something to others; to win a gold medal; a social trophy of some kind.

If they are salespeople, they tend to compare themselves against the 'greats', attend their lectures and seminars and try to put into place what only the 'greats' can do. It's the same as attending a lecture by an Olympic gold medallist. He can tell us what he does, what he thinks and how he trains, but despite our best efforts, many of us simply aren't built to win Olympic gold.

Moreover, comparing yourself to others must be the supreme folly. It's as foolish as comparing your house to some one else's because there will always be someone who has a better - and a worse - house than yours.

Who ever said that we have to live up to other peoples' expectations? Whoever said that the perfect shape for a human being is that of the current vogue?   Whoever said that there is only one success, and if you don't achieve it, you are a failure?

The culture we have created seems to regard only those who come first as 'winners'. This was demonstrated inadvertantly by the media during the 1992 Barcelona Olympics. Their reports on athletes who 'came second,' who 'will have to settle for a bronze' or worse, 'whose town will be disappointed' and so on were nothing short of disgraceful.

Surely anyone dedicated and talented enough to make the Olympics is a winner before he sets one foot in the stadium?

The attitude that only first place counts permeates our society. There are so many very talented people; executives, women wanting to re-enter the workforce, middle managers who haven't made it to Chief Executive Officer etc. who are still regarded by many as 'second raters'. Apart from anything else, that same attitude deprives our community of the best that many of these people have to offer.

It seems to me that Western society is not the font of all knowledge.   We haven't found all the answers, and a quick reference to events of the early nineties such as the Los Angeles riots, the tragedy of Somalia through Western inaction, the turmoil and human misery of Sarajevo and Gorazde, to name a few, will show that as a community we have a very long way to go before we can proclaim ourselves 'successful'.

I often think of the television image of a Colombian native who stood half-naked beside a river. The river was swollen yellow and coursed towards the sea carrying dead branches and swirling mud.

A close up of that native's face showed a profound serenity; a self-acceptance and satisfaction with life.   He knew every rock, tree, crevice, and mountain peak. He knew the clouds and the rain; the moist, leafy-green of the tropical forest; the bird calls and chatter of monkeys; the river; the birds and game.

He knew his village and his people; the laughter of children; the tears of old women. He knew that everything had a place, and he himself was part of the essential scheme of things with his own place and purpose in it.

What could I possibly tell that native about success? He is closer to life that most Westerners can ever hope to be. Yet about Wholistic success he could tell me a great deal.

It seems to me that few can ever achieve Wholistic success if they don't have understanding and acceptance of the following fundamentals:

- **Accept the society in which you live;** their faults and virtues. Change what you can and acknowledge what you can't change.

- **Live your own life.** Don't succumb to the social myths that abound everywhere. (E.g., in Australia there's the myth of the fit, bronzed, macho male who is expected to drink lots of beer and behave in a certain way. For women, there is the beauty myth propagated by cosmetics manufacturers, couturiers and slimming salons, etc) Every nation has their myths and trying to live up to them causes much misery. Be your own person.

- **Accept yourself.** You are built in a certain way; one perfect model of endless human variety.   Look around and you will see that we all come in different shapes and sizes. We all have particular aptitudes and skills. But we also have much in common: we breathe the same air, we need food and companionship to survive, we live on the same small planet and we all want a happy and safe future for our children.

- **Determine the success you want in all life's spheres.** Although this has been covered in depth, it bears repeating because of those people I mentioned earlier; those who seem to chase so feverishly after success but seldom catch it up. They equate success with money.

Equating success with money alone almost guarantees you will never achieve it.

- **Give yourself plenty of time and understanding.** We all experience highs and lows. If you had interviewed many of today's 'successes' in each year of their lives you would have found that for many of those years they were 'failures' in at least one sphere or another. There are years when you have money, and years when you don't. There might be times when you have a job, and times when you don't. So what?

  Success doesn't have time limits. Be gloriously and marvellously your own person and get the most from the success journey itself.

- **Remember that you won't be around forever.** Even though on 23 September 1992 Brisbane's Courier Mail carried a report that scientists are on the verge of unlocking the secrets of the 'aging' genes, making it possible for humans to live up to 400 years and still be 'young and fit', the central issue is still the quality - not the length - of the time we have.

So what about you?   Now that you have read The Personal Success Handbook what are you going to do with the rest of your life? Are you going to be like those who read such books and then put them aside without taking serious action? Who will simply go back to their routine and perhaps for a short while remember one or two thoughts?

Or will you be as those who ignore all the less convenient truths and focus on making money; without making the effort to set goals for your other life spheres; for more satisfying relationships, for working to build bridges between yourself and those who are 'less able' or 'less cultured'?

Am I going to meet you years from now only to find that where you are is the place in which you will be? Or will you grow in your stature as a more successful human being?

You are empowered to achieve wonderful things.

My wish for you is that you achieve that which is dearest to your heart. I want for you what you want. And if what I have shared with you in this book helps you achieve it even by a little, then I will rejoice because helping you succeed is part of my Wholistic success goal.

To your successful life.

Bibliography and Recommended Reading

MANZ, Charles C. & SIMS, Henry P. 'Superleadership'
New York. London. Toronto. Sydney. Tokyo.
Prentice Hall Press

HILL, N. 'Think and Grow Rich'
Hollywood Ca.,
Wilshire Book Company

HILL, N. 'Law of Success'
Evanston Illinois
Success Unlimited Inc.

HOPKINS, T 'How to Master the Art of Selling'
New York
Warner Books Inc.

FRANKLIN, Benjamin 'Franklin - The Autobiography'
by Daniel Aaron
New York USA
Vintage Books

KASSORLA, I. C. 'Go For It'
London
Futura Publications

STONE, W. C. 'Success Through a Positive Mental Attitude'
New York USA
Vintage Books

CARNEGIE, D 'How to Win Friends and Influence People'
North Ryde NSW Australia
Eden Paperbacks

CARNEGIE, D 'How to Stop Worrying and Start Living'
New York USA
Pocket Books

COHEN, H 'You Can Negotiate Anything'
North Ryde NSW Australia
Angus & Robertson Publishers

STANTON, H. E. 'The Success Factor'
Sydney
Collins Publishers Australia

SCHAEFER, H & 'A Guide to Public Speaking'
BRASHEAR, M. A. New York USA
The Berkley Publishing Group

CLASON, G. S. 'The Richest Man in Babylon'
New York USA
E. P. Dutton
Signet Books

PETERS, T. J. & 'In Search of Excellence'
WATERMAN Jr, R. H. New York. Sydney
Harper and Row Publishers

COVEY, S. R. 'The Seven Habits of Highly Effective People'
Melbourne.
The Business Library

JEFFERS, S. 'Feel the Fear and Do it Anyway'
London. Auckland. Johannesburgh.
Random Century Ltd

LAIRD, D. A. 'The Technique of Getting Things Done'
New York
McGraw Hill

MANDINO, O. **'The Greatest Salesman in the World'**
Hollywood Fla.,
Frederick Fell Publishers
Bantam Books

MALTZ, M. **'Psycho-Cybernetics'**
New York USA
Pocket Books

MITCHELL, S. **'Tall Poppies Too'**
Victoria.
Penguin Books Australia

BETTGER, F. **'How I Raised Myself from Failure to Success in Selling'**
New York USA
Simon Schuster Inc.

BETTGER, F. **'How I Multiplied My Income and Happiness in Selling'**
London UK
Ceder Books

McCORMACK, M. H. **'Success Secrets'**
Glasgow UK
William Collins Sons & Co Ltd

EYSENK, H. & **'Know Your Own Personality'**
WILSON, G. London UK
Maurice Temple Smith Ltd

ROHN, J. **'Seven Strategies for Wealth and Happiness'**
Rocklin CA.
Prima Publishing and Communications

MACKENZIE, A. **'The Time Trap'**
Melbourne VIC Australia
The Business Library

SCHWARTZ, D. J. **'The Magic of Thinking Big'**
Hollywood CA.
Wilshire Book Company

BERNE, E. **'Games People Play'**
Ringwood VIC Australia
Penguin Books

LEE-EMERY, B. **'Stop Procrastinating!'**
Milson's Point NSW Australia
Hutchinson Australia

VOGELAAR, D. M. **'How to Write a Business Plan'**
Melbourne VIC Australia
Australian Business Library

WATSON Jr, T. J. **'Father, Son and Co'**
New York. Toronto, London. Sydney. Auckland.
Bantam Books

MACKAY, H. **'How to Swim with the Sharks Without Being Eaten Alive'**
New York, Ivy Books

TRUMP, D. J. with **'The Art of the Deal'**
SCHWARTZ, T. Hawthorn Australia, Auckland N.Z.,
Bergvlei, South Africa
Century Hutchinson